The Miracle of Kayla

God's Perfect Timing

DANIEL J. WILLIAMS

WESTBOW
PRESS®
A DIVISION OF THOMAS NELSON
& ZONDERVAN

Copyright © 2018 Daniel J. Williams.

All rights reserved. No part of this book may be used or reproduced by any means, graphic, electronic, or mechanical, including photocopying, recording, taping or by any information storage retrieval system without the written permission of the author except in the case of brief quotations embodied in critical articles and reviews.

This book is a work of non-fiction. Unless otherwise noted, the author and the publisher make no explicit guarantees as to the accuracy of the information contained in this book and in some cases, names of people and places have been altered to protect their privacy.

Scriptures taken from the Holy Bible, New International Version®, NIV®. Copyright © 1973, 1978, 1984, 2011 by Biblica, Inc.™ Used by permission of Zondervan. All rights reserved worldwide. www.zondervan.com The "NIV" and "New International Version" are trademarks registered in the United States Patent and Trademark Office by Biblica, Inc.™

WestBow Press books may be ordered through booksellers or by contacting:

WestBow Press
A Division of Thomas Nelson & Zondervan
1663 Liberty Drive
Bloomington, IN 47403
www.westbowpress.com
1 (866) 928-1240

Because of the dynamic nature of the Internet, any web addresses or links contained in this book may have changed since publication and may no longer be valid. The views expressed in this work are solely those of the author and do not necessarily reflect the views of the publisher, and the publisher hereby disclaims any responsibility for them.

Any people depicted in stock imagery provided by Getty Images are models, and such images are being used for illustrative purposes only. Certain stock imagery © Getty Images.

ISBN: 978-1-9736-3103-3 (sc)
ISBN: 978-1-9736-3104-0 (hc)
ISBN: 978-1-9736-3102-6 (e)

Library of Congress Control Number: 2018907001

Print information available on the last page.

WestBow Press rev. date: 06/29/2018

"Unless they have experienced it for themselves, few couples can understand the heartache that comes from the inability to conceive a child. Dan Williams' book paints an emotional picture of that pain, but also reminds readers of the comfort that comes from knowing God will meet them at their point of need."

> Jim Daly, President – Focus on the Family
> Foreword by U.S. Senator James Lankford

CONTENTS

Dedication ix

Acknowledgements...xi

Foreword..xiii

Disclaimer.. xv

Introduction... xvii

Chapter 1   The Beginning of an Odyssey 1

Chapter 2   My Better Half 15

Chapter 3   The Supporting Cast...............................26

Chapter 4   The Unexpected Detour......................... 31

Chapter 5   A Prayer Answered.................................44

Chapter 6   God's Will 50

Chapter 7   One More Try 55

Chapter 8   Getting off the Canvas...........................60

Chapter 9   "Mariah" 69

Chapter 10   May 26, 2011...76

Chapter 11   The Long Night 88

Chapter 12   A Parade of Possible Victims 94

Chapter 13   Boxing with God 102

Chapter 14   God Can Make a Way 105

Chapter 15   The Interview of a Lifetime................. 111

Chapter 16   The Wait... 118

Chapter 17   The Easiest Decision I Ever Made 126

Chapter 18   The Miracle...129

Chapter 19 My Last Day 137
Chapter 20 Lessons from a Child 141
Chapter 21 My Final Thoughts 152

Afterword 157
About the Author 161

DEDICATION

This book is dedicated to my wife Nancy, who helped inspire this story, and to Kayla, who will own my heart forever. I would also like to dedicate it to all those couples struggling with infertility, birth mothers considering adoption as an alternative, and to adoption agencies like Nightlight Christian Adoption, who seek to provide birth mothers with an alternative for their unborn child.

I would also like to acknowledge my parents who developed in me the moral compass that helped guide my life in the tough times, and my sister Mary who always had my back.

I would be remiss if I did not express my gratitude to the men and women of John Butchee's Sunday school class at Southern Hills Baptist Church. Their constant prayers and encouragement helped us to keep our eyes and hearts focused on God's faithfulness.

Finally, I would like to dedicate this book to my Federal Bureau of Investigation (FBI) family, especially the Oklahoma City Division, whose unwavering support was instrumental to this story.

ACKNOWLEDGEMENTS

The DNA of this book was influenced by the support and guidance of the following people:

1. Megan Marie Cox, an accomplished published author who helped me to navigate the publishing world and how to even write a book. It also didn't hurt that her husband, Casey, was one of the heroes of the book.
2. Kay McAndrew, whose amazing ability to search out the beauty and clarity of the English language, helped give breath to my words and life to the pages between the cover of this book.
3. My long-time friend Margaret Finegan, whose keen eyes previously scoured through numerous tax returns with the Internal Revenue Service for nearly forty years, helped keep my words concise and thoughts focused.

FOREWORD

I had the pleasure of first meeting Dan Williams, and several other FBI agents who worked directly for him, during my first congressional campaign. Their friendship and humor shattered the stereotype of the stiff, no-nonsense FBI agent often portrayed in movies. They personified the FBI's motto of fidelity, bravery and integrity.

I was there when Dan and Nancy became the victims of an adoption fraud. I saw the pain and anguish they endured to have a child. Nevertheless, their faith in God's mercy and love never wavered.

Dan's story is a beautifully told narrative of faith in a loving God who does the impossible daily around and through ordinary people. He describes in heart-wrenching detail his and Nancy's seven-year struggle with infertility, the loss of their first child through a miscarriage, the difficulties of trying to adopt, and a life-shattering adoption fraud. Yet it is a statement of God's incredible faithfulness and power to overcome the difficulties we all experience at some time in our lives, even when we battle doubt and despair.

It was evident that God had prepared them for this painful journey, but as you read you will feel the pain and loss. His story is peppered with many personal accounts of his own father who would help establish the foundation for his life and anecdotes about the FBI. Each day of his past was part of God's plan and preparation

xiii

for the future. Entwined in every page is God's love, mercy and faithfulness. The kind of faith that led to *The Miracle of Kayla*.

James Lankford
United States Senator

DISCLAIMER

The following account is my own personal description of events based upon my best recollection. Embedded in every page is my own personal faith. The story is not so much about me or my family, but how I believe God used us to tell his story.

The opinions expressed within these pages are mine and not those of the Federal Bureau of Investigation.

INTRODUCTION

Even after more than two decades in the Federal Bureau of Investigation (FBI), I never realized the biggest heartbreak and triumph in my life would start and end right inside my own home. I spent my career working some of the FBI's top profile cases from chasing down top ten fugitives to traveling the world to prevent terrorist events back home. The FBI Academy at Quantico, Virginia, had prepared me for many things, but it never equipped me for the journey my wife Nancy and I departed on to have the child we believed God had placed on our hearts.

It was an expedition I certainly would not have chosen for my wife and me. It was a seven-year journey that seemed more like a roller coaster ride through hope and despair.

The pain, emptiness and heartache that comes with the desire to have a child, only to be confronted by the impassable wall of infertility, is difficult to fathom for those who are blessed with the ability to conceive. Mother's Day and Father's Day serve as additional reminders of the empty void in your life. Eventually, they become days on the calendar you look to with dread. Baby showers are difficult events that serve to remind you of the hole in your own heart and the difficulty it takes to smile when jealousy is consuming your spirit. The coo and laughter of a baby only serve as a microphone for the pain echoing in the abyss of your soul.

Yet we were about to learn God will sometimes take you to places you never imagined going. Yes, sometimes the walk can be

xvii

painful, but the destination is always better than anyone could have ever imagined.

The story I want to tell is not so much about myself or family, but the story of how God interceded in our lives in our darkest hour when we lost all hope. It is simply God's story, and we were given the honor to be characters in it.

I hope that somewhere in this story you may see pieces of your own story tucked in between the pages. Perhaps the challenges you might be struggling with concerning doubt and faith, or when you are overcome by despair as you wonder why God has forsaken you.

Yet God weaves the tapestry of his stories long before we ever realize it. This story began with a man who God placed in my life as a young boy. A man who would become the benchmark for who I wanted to be and who would place the compass in my hand to seek my true north in God. The man who ignited my own fire to one day be a father, and whose words God would use to prepare me for the challenges that awaited me.

CHAPTER 1

The Beginning of an Odyssey

"You are all set to go, Agent Williams," said the officer who initialed the log. I retrieved my badge and credentials from his hands. I then placed them in my suit coat jacket as I prepared to leave the law enforcement checkpoint at the airport in Washington, D.C.

Prior to my departure, he inquired, "What is the award you are carrying?"

"It is the Director's Award," I replied. "It is the highest award you can receive from the FBI."

"Wow, what did you get it for?"

"A counterterrorism investigation that prevented a terrorist organization from smuggling shoulder-fire weapons into the United States (U.S.) to bring down commercial aircraft."

"Wow! Thanks," he replied. "I am sure all of us working in airports will appreciate that kind of case!"

I just smiled, turned away, and walked out into the terminal. I was privileged to have been a part of the investigation, but the truth was the case was initiated by a handful of tenacious and dedicated agents from the Newark FBI Division such as James

1

Tareco, Chris Settembrino, Laura Robinson, Frank Ventura, Kevin Kline and several others. These agents sacrificed unbelievable hours and experienced personal hardship to follow every possible lead and angle to prevent an attack that could have conceivably taken thousands of American lives.

My part was small in comparison. I was assigned to spearhead the international efforts from FBI headquarters (FBIHQ), which involved working with international law enforcement and intelligence officers around the world. Together, we would travel to various places around the world.

As the highest-ranking agent from FBIHQ at the table, I was responsible for negotiating the investigative strategy with our international partners. Yet, I also knew that tact and diplomacy were not my strong suit. I had more of a reputation for being a bull in a china shop and subsequently feared being more a detriment than an asset to the case. I often thank Special Agent (SA) Michael McCall for preventing me from causing an international incident. His outstanding command of foreign languages and customs kept me from putting my foot in my mouth more than once.

This case necessitated constant updates and briefings to the director, attorney general, and eventually the president. It also caused me a great deal of frustration dealing with the FBIHQ bureaucracy. I often joked if I could just get past the good guys, getting the bad guys would be easy. Nevertheless, the privilege of working with these outstanding professionals was one of the many highlights of my FBI career. Their excellent work resulted in the successful prosecution of this terrorist organization.

Now I found my gate heading back home to Oklahoma City. I was going to have to wait several hours before we could board. I had traveled so often with the FBI that I grew to hate airports, especially international flights. It was always hurry up and wait. But this flight would be unlike any other, and it would start a journey I never saw coming.

Rather than sit there bored waiting for my plane, I bought a

The Miracle of Kayla

newspaper and sat down at a restaurant to eat and read since I had plenty of time. Yet there was a restlessness in my heart I just couldn't shake. I had carried it with me since I had left home in Oklahoma City a few days earlier. Yet for whatever reason, I just couldn't place my finger on what was troubling me. I had just received the Director's Award with all the pageantry and honor that went with it, but something was still missing in my life.

By this point in my career, I had received many awards including the FBI Shield of Bravery and the Organized Crime Drug Enforcement Task Force Case of the Year award. I had also been a two-time recipient of the National Federal Law Enforcement Officers Association Achievement Award. This new award should have been the highlight of my career. Instead, it was just another paperweight I had to lug home. Yet, I just couldn't put my finger on what was bothering me.

After I ate, I picked up the paper to read, but my eyes caught sight of a young father teaching his son how to play chess on a small chessboard while they waited for their flight. I put the paper down and started to watch them interact. Suddenly, my mind flashed back to another time and place when I was young.

"Know where you are going and how you are going to get there." Words I would often hear my father say just as we would sit down to play chess. It was his feeble attempt to use psychological warfare to gain some advantage over me. Throughout the game, he would look at me and say, "If you want to be successful in chess or life, you have to develop a strategic plan and learn how to think outside the box."

He had taught me how to play the game when I was just a ten-year-old child. It was a game I took to immediately. After only three games, I beat him, and he would never beat me again. Dad had always fancied himself a chess aficionado in the navy. Now he was suffering the indignity of being shown-up consistently by his ten-year-old son.

Every win was followed by my customary victory dance around the table. I guess it was my way of advertising who was the new

3

Daniel J. Williams

alpha male in the pack. He would just smile and shake his head. Dad realized to his chagrin, for better or worse, I was my father's son. But it was those simple words of "thinking outside the box" that would have such an impact later on in my life.

A short time later, I watched the father and his son in the airport fold up the chessboard. They were scrambling to get all their bags and suitcases together. In the background, I could see a woman waving them on. Before they could pack away the chessboard, the small box came open, and the chess pieces fell to the floor. The woman in the background was shaking her head in disgust. The father, sensing he was about to get lectured, quickly retrieved the pieces and placed them in the box. The son hurried off to meet his frustrated mother at the gate. His dad was left to carry all the bags. I couldn't help but laugh.

I then leaned back into my chair. I had not thought about my own father in some time. Work always found a way to consume my life, leaving me little time to think about the past. It was a pleasure I rarely indulged in. Yet as I propped back into my chair, my mind continued to drift back to another era in my life and to the man who helped shape it.

Dad and I shared so many interests including football, baseball, and sneaking off together to eat fried clams. He even spent time teaching me how to box, which seemed appropriate, since I spent so much of my time getting into fights. His cousin would later tell me my father had a reputation for getting into many fights during his career in the navy. My father's cousin confessed he started most of them leaving my father to clean-up the mess. Apparently, Dad never backed down from any of the fights, even when he was outnumbered. I guess it was a family trait I would inherit.

Whenever I played Little League baseball, I would search out the crowd looking for his approving nod in the stand. Somehow, just knowing he was there made me feel better about stepping up to the plate.

My father was more than just a mentor; he was my best friend.

4

The Miracle of Kayla

How I would love to play catch, eat clams, or go to Fenway Park to see the Red Sox with him. Often our conversations would deviate from the games to general conversations about life. What I didn't realize at the time, and perhaps he didn't either, was that our conversations were slowly seeding the values that would become the compass for my life.

We talked about God, family, country, my responsibility as the eldest son, and what I wanted to be when I grew up. Naturally, I wanted to be just about everything, such as a ball player, a fighter, an army officer (mainly because he was enlisted navy, and I knew it would stoke his ire), and an FBI agent.

It was being an FBI agent that seemed to raise his curiosity the most. He would often ask me what I knew about the FBI. What were the requirements to be an agent, and what steps did I plan on taking to become an agent?

At ten years old, I had no clue how to answer any of those questions. He would put his arm around me, tousle my hair, and say the same words I would hear before every chess game, "Know where you are going and how you are going to get there. Remember Danny, life is a lot like chess. You have to be prepared to make the sacrifices."

Yet, what I really wanted to tell him was all I wanted to be was him. He was my hero and measuring stick. Sadly, I never got to tell him that in his lifetime. How many times I regretted that omission in my own life.

Oh, my father was anything but perfect. He could often appear very gruff until he relaxed his guard. In fact, he could be hard to reach at times. He was career navy and a veteran of World War II, the Korean War, and the Vietnam War. Often I would try to engage him in conversation about his time in the war, but he would rarely ever discuss it.

The Promise I Made to Myself

In all our years together, I can only recall one time that he ever said he loved me. I was approximately eleven years old at the time. I am not sure exactly what I said or did, but I was acting my usual sarcastic self when he reached over and slapped me on the back of the head. That slap sent me flying halfway across the room. He immediately ran over, picked me up, held me close to his chest, and said, "I'm so sorry. I wasn't trying to hurt you. All I wanted was to get your attention. Danny, I love you son, but I'm not going to stand around and let you say inappropriate things about anyone."

I wish I remembered what I said that infuriated him so much, but this was the first time my father ever embraced me, or said he loved me. Oh, in my heart I always knew it. I never questioned it once. Yet, it was nice to finally hear it even if it meant getting slapped. Naturally, I couldn't let him see me getting teary-eyed. So I wiped my nose, stepped back, and jokingly said he was lucky I wasn't five pounds heavier. (I was lucky if I was eighty pounds. He was 6'1" and over 200 pounds.) He just reached out for me and held me again. In turn, I held onto his neck. How I cherished that embrace. Yet, I promised myself years later that my child would never long to hear the words "I love you." He or she would hear it until I took my last breath.

God and Country

In my father's world view, a man was supposed to be strong, unemotional, fearless, and ready to solve any problem at any time. He maintained strict discipline, and heaven help us if we crossed the line. Even when he taught Bible school to a high school class, he would not accept anything less than the very best from his students. If they failed to know an answer when he called upon them in class, he would make them get down and do pushups. Yet, even though

The Miracle of Kayla

he came off more as a drill sergeant than a Sunday school teacher, his students loved him.

My father only knew one way to do things — the navy way. The old chief petty officer, battle-tested by three wars, developed his value system through a military tradition that demanded the ultimate sacrifice when called upon. After he enlisted in the navy, he was immediately assigned to the Pacific Theater during World War II alongside his father. His brother, my uncle Fred, was also career navy.

When he would discuss my future, it always started after I went to college and joined the military. (In my ten-year-old mind, it always started after my induction into the NFL Hall of Fame.) He could never imagine my life being lived without having served my country. I knew this was the backdrop of how he would measure my success as a man once I grew up.

Church was never an option in my father's life, nor would he let it be in mine. Often, either before or after work, he would stop by church just to pray. Sometimes before we would sneak off to get our fried clams, he would step into church with me in tow to say a quick prayer. Afterwards, he would utter something to the effect, "Church is just a good place to go to clear your mind." If there was something weighing heavy on him, he would never tell me. What he did not realize at the time, nor did I, was that his son was slowly learning through osmosis where a man should go when life was pressing on him.

The Rambunctious Son

These high expectations he held for himself were also demanded of me. He was fully aware his son could be a bit rambunctious at times, but he had no one to blame for that except himself. He understood all too well, for better or worse, I had taken on many of his character traits. Nevertheless, he made me search out the

7

Daniel J. Williams

very best I could be in whatever endeavor I took on, even if I didn't necessarily enjoy it. Average was unacceptable.

"Life," my father would declare each time I found myself on the wrong side of his ledger, "is about growing and learning. It is about finding your place, and being the best you can be. It is not about trying to be better than other people. It is about being better than who you were yesterday. Failure is not losing; it is giving up. Son, you need to start learning from your mistakes, and if you are even smarter, you will learn from the mistakes of others as well. This way you won't live in the vicious cycle of making the same mistake over and over again. Danny, this world is not going to hand you what you want. You have to earn it. There are no shortcuts. It comes through hard work and sweat. Now wake up before I have to ground you again."

I can't count how many times I heard this speech, especially when my report card was not stellar. I'm not sure how much of it resonated with me in my early life because I kept repeating the same mistakes. Now I often wonder how much of it was meant for the boy back then, or the man I one day would become.

Yet, I had a way of getting away with things no one else could. When he would finally get annoyed with my constant antics, he would bellow out, "Knock it off before I come over and knock you off. Listen kid, I brought you into this world, and I can take you out of it if you don't straighten up."

My retort would usually be, "Dad, Mom brought me into this world, not you. I don't recall seeing you when I made my grand entrance into this world. Mom claims you were not even there at the hospital."

He would do his best not to laugh at this ten-year-old smart aleck who was deliberately testing his patience. There was little doubt he was amused by this little eighty-pound upstart who would challenge his authority. He often reminded me that if one of his enlisted sailors had acted like I did, he would make him walk the plank.

The Miracle of Kayla

This only elicited amusement on my part. "Dad," I would quip, "you would have to catch me first. You just need to face the fact you are not fast enough."

His comeback was always, "Every cub has to return to the den to eat. I don't have to go anywhere, but I assure you there is a belt waiting just for you with your name on it when you get home."

Alas, the young, pugnacious warrior inside of me knew it was time to raise the white flag. This would usually end our exchange of wit. He had me, and I knew it. More importantly, he knew it too. Checkmate!

The Life of Balance

Years later, while we were waiting for clams to be delivered to our table, my father leaned back in his chair with his arms folded in front of him. I could tell something was on his mind.

"Dad, what's up?"

"I worry about you. You are extremely driven, but sometimes you can be shortsighted. I fear you might miss out on what is really important while chasing the prize."

"So, Dad, are you telling me to strive for mediocrity?"

He smiled and laughed. "No, Danny. I just want you to know that life is more than living for the conquest. Victory can be short-lived. It can sometimes cause you to lose sight of all the wonderful things God has placed right in front of you. Live your life for the things that last for eternity by learning to live in the moment, and giving thanks to God for all that he has given you. Life is too short, and you will never get a second chance to buy back today. You need to make sure you use God's will as your measuring stick."

"Well, Dad, when those clams arrive on the table, I will be living in the moment. Unfortunately, they are not going to last forever, and if you turn away, neither are yours."

He just smiled and shook his head. I knew he was trying to tell

Daniel J. Williams

me something important, but it was just too deep to grasp. Yet, this little conversation, which never really matured into what my father was hoping to finish, would later resonate in my mind hundreds of times. Over the years, through the fire of adversity and heartache, I came to understand he was talking about finding a balance in my life. While he had only been able to initiate the conversation, God would complete the lesson.

Time to Go

Suddenly, I could hear the flight attendant call my flight overhead. I paid the bill and ran to the gate. After being walked down the ramp by the flight attendant since I was armed, I introduced myself to the pilot. After looking me over several times and asking what seemed like a hundred questions, I took a seat.

In my customary way, I looked at the faces of every passenger who passed me. Experience had taught me how to read faces and to look for possible trouble, but fortunately, it didn't appear I was likely to have any trouble on this flight.

Coming down the aisle was a father carrying his three-year-old girl. "Daddy, I three," was the big investigative clue I used to determine her age.

"Yes you are sweetheart," as he hugged her tight and their cheeks embraced.

As the plane started to take off, I could see how excited she was. I surmised this was her first flight. I could tell she was the apple of her father's eyes. I saw his enjoyment as he looked down to see the wonder in his daughter's eyes as she tried to capture everything happening outside the window. Yet as I looked at her, I was amazed at how much she looked like my sister, Mary Ann, at the same age.

When we finally reached our cruising altitude, I closed my eyes hoping to pass time on the two-hour flight. Soon my mind was drifting back to my father.

The Image Forever Engrained

Dad remained this hard, strong, unbreakable figure in my life until the day we adopted my baby sister as an infant. Suddenly, this big bear of a man turned to mush. She was the apple of his eye. He would sit there for hours cooing back at my sister as he bounced her off of his knee. When he fed her, he started off by pretending the spoon was a navy plane taking off from an aircraft carrier in the Pacific. She would smile and laugh. He would then place the spoon in her mouth while she was smiling from ear to ear.

When she was three years, he would take her with us when we threw around the football. He would place my helmet on her head and pretend she was our center as he would send me out for a pass. She in turn would put the helmet on the ground with her head still in it and her little butt in the air. He would break out laughing, pick her up, then throw her up in the air and catch her. She would burst out laughing. "Again, Daddy," she would cry out. Once again, he would throw her back up in the air, and the two of them would continue laughing as he would hold her with their faces pressed together.

I would stand there with my football in my hand, after making a great catch which would have been featured on any NFL highlight reel, watching my little sister turn my bear-like father into her little play toy. Whether or not she realized it, she had him wrapped around her little finger. However, the attention he showered on her never bothered me. It only served to soften his tough image and gave me a deeper understanding of the man.

He had spent most of my early childhood at sea. Now was his opportunity to be around to see one of his children grow up, starting as a baby. How he relished every moment. The image of them together, as he tossed her in the air, was fixed in my mind long into my adulthood. The old chief petty officer had made many sacrifices in his life. He had missed out on many of the important things that he knew he could never reclaim, and he was determined not to let it slip through his fingers again.

Dad had finally found the "balance" he had so often pressed me to embrace. He found it in his family. He would also find it in one other place, but I would not discover it until God would take me on my own seven-year journey through heartache and despair. A journey that would lead me to a place where I stood totally humbled before God.

However, on the day after Christmas, the man who helped shape my values lost his life to a heart attack. I kept begging him to go outside to throw my new football around, but this time, the ball lacked the hard spirals he usually threw. A short time later, we went back inside, and not long afterwards, he fell from our couch. Sometime during the ambulance ride to the hospital, he passed away.

At his funeral a few days later, I tried to stand at attention with my hand over my heart the way he taught me whenever taps was being played. Only this time as the bugle played, my heart was heavy as I stood there trying to be brave in the cold wind. It was then I noticed my clip-on tie had fallen off. Yet, my embarrassment was overshowed by my sense of loss. My body trembled with the sound of each rifle volley. As they folded the flag draped coffin, I could only grieve the man who would no longer be there to shape my life.

When they presented the flag to my mother, my tears started to roll. It was then my Uncle Fred, and his wife, my Aunt Jackie, placed their hands on my shoulder. How much it meant to have them there to support us.

I was a young boy reaching the point where I needed my father the most. Now, more than ever, I needed my dad. Was I ready to go forth from this point on without him?

Nevertheless, our conversations would point the way many times later in my life. God had given me my father for only a short season to start my journey on this road called life. But in that time, God had used my father to teach me many things and to forge in me the values that would shape my life. Long before God sets us out on a journey, he equips us with the tools we need to complete it. In my case, it started with a man who cared enough about me to stand beside me, and in some cases, in front of me.

God's New Purpose for My Life

In what seemed like a brief minute, the flight attendant was announcing that we would be making our descent into Oklahoma City. "Please turn off all electronic devices and move your seat-backs forward," she said over the intercom. Suddenly, I felt a tear drop as I had relived my father's life in a few hours.

As I gazed out the window at the city below, I had spent most of this trip looking back at my life. God had given me a great life and a blessed marriage with Nancy. I had accomplished so much in my life, but it was not because of who I was. In fact, it was in spite of who I was. Yet, something still seemed to be missing. Suddenly, I found myself whispering, "God, what do you want me to do with the rest of the life you have given me." While there was no burning bush revelation, I suddenly felt God press gently on my heart, "Be a father." It was the same question I had posed to God prior to leaving FBIHQ in 2004. The answer had not changed. His answer was not to be a great leader, FBI agent, Nobel laureate, athlete, or accomplished politician. It was simply being a dad.

Unfortunately, like so many times in my life, I failed to heed his call. How often I would run when I would hear the siren's call of work, but slow-walk, or even turn a deaf ear to the silent, clear whisper of God. Yet it stirred my heart this time and provided me with a new dream of the father I wanted to be. The type of father God was now calling me to be. God had already blessed me with a great example when I was a child. I could not wait to get home to discuss what I felt God had placed on my heart. What I didn't understand at the moment as I disembarked the flight was God was going to place Nancy and me on a new journey. A journey I never saw coming.

My father, Claude J. Williams and me.

CHAPTER 2

My Better Half

I was standing at the baggage claim area when I met a young U.S. Army captain. He had already experienced more than men twice his age. He had just returned from Iraq, and he was hoping to take command of a company size unit soon. While we waited for the luggage to start rolling through, I briefly told him about my experience as a company commander when I was a young army captain many years earlier. When my luggage arrived, I shook his hand and thanked him for his service.

After retrieving my suitcase from the baggage claim area, I started to head for my car, but I turned around for a second to look back at the young man I just met. Despite the fact we barely knew each other, I was proud of this young man. He had the courage and conviction to commit himself to a cause greater than himself. As he stood there panning the luggage belt for his duffle bag, it hit me like a rock. While I never achieved my boyhood dream of being inducted into the Football Hall of Fame, I had unwittingly accomplished the two goals my father had envisioned for my future. I completed college including graduate school, and served in the military. I had somehow measured up to his benchmark in spite of myself.

Maybe this trip down memory lane was God's way of speaking

Daniel J. Williams

to me. In just a short flight, I was now fully invested in the plan I believed God laid out before me to be a father.

By this time the gun was digging into my side. I couldn't wait to shed it and this award I had been lugging around all day. How I longed to get back home to my wife. Soon I was back in my car heading home. I wanted to tell Nancy about the desire God placed on my heart to have a child. Would she feel the same excitement I was feeling? Would she feel as invested in God's plan as I was? We had previously talked about children and had tried for two years. However, my job always got in the way.

When I was promoted to FBIHQ years earlier, I was eventually placed in charge of a counterterrorism unit. My day would often begin around 4:30 a.m., and I wouldn't get home most days until 10 p.m. I was also frequently traveling to many places. If we got time on the weekends to go to dinner or the movies, it was interrupted with phone calls from the FBI. Often I could not tell her anything about what I was doing, or where I was traveling.

All this could have been a recipe for divorce, but Nancy was my blessing from God. She was a beautiful, gregarious blonde who was very focused, driven, self-confident, and smart. Wow was she smart! She was her high school's class valedictorian and thrived while in college, earning her Doctor of Pharmacy degree from the University of Michigan. I would jokingly tell her I was the 1% that made the top 99% possible. I was just happy to have a degree.

We often joked we likely would never have dated each other in high school. Yet what attracted me the most was how sweet she was. She was a woman of deep faith and conviction. She was the most honest person I ever knew. More importantly, she actually found something in me that allowed her to see the man behind the crazy job. I never had to try to impress her or be anything other than myself.

When I pulled into the driveway, she was waiting for me at the door. She threw her arms around my neck and said, "Wow, I have missed you. I want to hear every detail about your awards ceremony

16

The Miracle of Kayla

and trip!" Nancy couldn't make the trip with me because of a prior commitment that she couldn't cancel.

"It was all great," I replied. "I caught up with a lot of old friends, and it was nice to see my family. And as always, the best view of Washington, D.C. was in my rearview mirror. But what I really want to talk with you about was my incredible journey home."

"What could be more exciting than to receive the Director's Award?"

"God placed something on my heart, and now I want to share it with you." I then told her about my trip down memory lane and how the flight seemed over before it got started. "Nancy, I think God is telling us it is time to have a baby."

She sat there next to me with a puzzled look on her face. I wasn't sure if she thought I had lost my mind on the trip, or I was just misinterpreting a memory of my father for a calling to be a father.

"Wow! Sweetheart, for the last several days I had been having the same thought. Do you really think God could be giving us a sign it is time to have our own child?"

"Nancy, I don't think I have ever been more certain of anything in my whole life!"

We then spent the next several hours talking about our future, a child and expanding our family. We were convinced that since we had now been reassigned to Oklahoma, we would have more time to actually try to have children. Soon we allowed our imagination to run away with us. Yet, we also talked about the many sacrifices we would have to make. A child would require many changes in our lifestyle, but we were ready to do whatever was necessary. This was something both of us wanted. It was a lifetime commitment we were obligating our lives to. A child would be an amazing blessing from God. A blessing that would come with an overwhelming sense of responsibility.

Naturally, like most couples, we had differing opinions at times especially when it came to names, but it was still exciting to talk

17

Daniel J. Williams

about it. We lost all track of time that night, and soon it was time to go to sleep.

Nancy was now asleep and snoring like a bear, but I was still restless. I was jealous of the gift she had to fall asleep in the blink of an eye. Yet as I watched her easily drift into her deep slumber, I couldn't help but think how blessed I was to have her in my life. She would make a wonderful mother. As I nestled under the blanket, I laid there contemplating whether our meeting was really just an accident or the divine providence of God.

My New Friend

When I went apartment hunting in Monroe, Louisiana, I had narrowed my search down to three apartment complexes. The next day, I went to put my deposit on the apartment I liked the most, but another individual rented the apartment. My second choice was also rented out the previous night. When I arrived at final choice the manager also informed me she had just rented out the apartment. However, she informed me she had another apartment that had just become available, but it didn't have the greatest view. When she took me to see it, she was correct. The only view was the back of a busy store with trucks coming and going all day. But I was desperate. It was cheap, and at least I wouldn't have to be there all day because my job would ensure I remained busy.

A few days later, I started up the stairs to my apartment when my eye caught this beautiful girl sitting on the porch reading a book. We briefly exchanged pleasantries, and I learned her name was Nancy. She was an associate professor at the College of Pharmacy and my next door neighbor. She also introduced me to her dog Nebba. Unbeknownst to me, her dog was very sick. We made small talk for a little while until I heard the phone ringing in my apartment. It was the FBI calling as usual.

The Miracle of Kayla

A few days later, I saw her early one morning standing outside crying as she coddled her very small dog in her arms.

"Nancy, are you all right?"

She could barely speak through all the tears streaming down her cheek. "Could you take a picture of me and Nebba? I would like one last picture of us together. I have to take her to the vet to be put to sleep." She struggled to get each word out and had to pause at times to catch her breath. Now the dam of tears had broken, and she was sobbing. She stood there looking at me helplessly.

"I would be happy to. Why don't you sit down in your living room, and I will take the picture inside?" She complied with my suggestion, and I took several pictures for her.

"Thank you so much," she whimpered as we walked out of her apartment.

I felt really sad for her. I could see she was very attached to the dog. Not really sure of the appropriate thing to say, I blurted out, "I hope you feel better after Nebuchadnezzar is comfortably resting paws up."

When I got into my car and started to drive away, it hit me like a rock. Good grief! Paws Up! Did I really just say that? I didn't even remember the correct name of her dog! I sounded like a typical mob guy taking some other thug for his final ride. How could I even begin to apologize for being such a jerk!

I immediately turned around to apologize, but her car was gone when I returned to the parking lot. I was determined to leave work early for once so I could make amends; however, when I returned home, she was not there.

A few hours later, she knocked on my door. I was certain she had come over to tell me what an idiot I was, but instead she apologized for being such a mess that morning. She wanted me to know how thankful she was that I was there to take one last picture of her with her dog. I immediately offered up a counter-apology if I said anything that might have upset her.

19

Daniel J. Williams

"I'm sorry if I wasn't listening. I could only focus on Nebba," she said with a bewildered look.

Wow, I had dodged a bullet. I was just going to keep my mouth shut and go with the moment. I walked her back to her apartment and told her to call if she needed anything.

The Unforeseen First Kiss

Even though I lived next door to her, we initially didn't get to see a lot of each other. Work kept us very busy. But occasionally, I would come back home and see her sitting outside reading or preparing for lectures. We would sit on the steps for hours getting caught up in our conversations. She had just received her tenure at the University of Louisiana at Monroe College of Pharmacy. We shared many of the same philosophical, political and religious viewpoints. There was no topic we couldn't talk or laugh about. At the same time, she wasn't afraid to call me out. More importantly, she was unattached.

However, there was one problem I just couldn't get around — she was my next door neighbor. I could not date the girl next door. It was simply too close. I immediately established a new rule for my life — *never date your next door neighbor.* This new rule would establish a boundary around my life I would not cross. If things went sour, I would be the one who would have to move. I could never let anything remotely romantic happen between us.

Still, I would often bump into her on the steps or at the pool. I relished our conversations. Soon, we had a blossoming friendship, and I was sharing things with her I wouldn't share with most people. One day I asked her if she wanted to go to the movies "just as friends." Then we went to the hockey games, college football games, and often played mini-golf "just as friends." Wherever we went, I would always pick up the tab and open her door. I would always emphasize in our conversations I was not looking for a romantic relationship. All I wanted was a friend.

The Miracle of Kayla

Nancy and I miniature golfing on a "non-date".

However, I was scared to death of getting romantically involved. Somehow my job would always get in the way. Inevitably, I would get hurt when they would leave because they wanted someone who would put them first over the badge. I could hardly blame them. But more importantly, I didn't want to hurt someone else. It was just easier at this point in my life to be friends. This way I wouldn't have to play games, try to be witty, or engage in the drama dating often created. I could just be me, or so I thought.

My new friend was also becoming my chief competitor. She turned everything into a competition whether it was a card game, golf, bowling, monopoly, mini-golf or any other sport. I had always been an athlete and took great pride in my physical conditioning. Since I was a young teenager, I had been an accomplished martial artist and boxer. I was competing and winning matches consistently. Eventually, I would even take home the National Lightweight title. I often maxed out the physical fitness test in the military and at the

Daniel J. Williams

FBI Academy in Quantico. If I was not working, you could always find me at the gym. It was my home away from home.

Yet when it came to a physical competition, she was not intimidated by any of my athletic achievements. The first time we played tennis I thought I would go easy on her. Unfortunately, she forgot to tell me she had been a competitive tennis player since high school. I could barely return her serve, and if I did, she would hit the ball to every place I wasn't. I was exhausted, but I was never going to let her have the satisfaction of knowing it. Finally, after being trounced after three sets, I was mentally ready to throw in the towel.

"Not such a tough guy after all!"

"Hey," as I was huffing and puffing to get my words out, "didn't you learn in your psychology classes in college that the male ego is a very fragile thing. I'm not sure I have one left. Whatever I still had is missing in action somewhere out there on the court."

"Buck up tough guy. You honestly didn't think we were done yet. I thought all you FBI guys were supposed to be real macho types. What happened?"

"Any machismo I had was shattered by a girl who gave me no mercy."

"I'm sorry. I will be gentler with your fragile little ego next time. I would hate to be responsible for beating up on a poor, feeble FBI agent. Besides, who is going to protect us weak and helpless girls if we don't have you out there on the street protecting us. Now come on. We are just beginning."

Ouch! Now I was barely standing up with my hands on my knees supporting my weight. I was perspiring profusely as my chest was trying to catch one last breath. I was looking at this nutty girl bouncing up and down on the tennis court delighting in the certain prospect of delivering another crushing defeat.

Okay, any male machismo I had was now gone, but that made this "thing" between us even more interesting. What this "thing" was I could not say, but I was falling hard for it.

So for the next year, we were "just friends." I would always

22

introduce her as "my friend Nancy." But even my best friend and boss Sam Macaluso would give me that look at times and say, "I think you are the only one who believes that."

One Friday evening, I took my friend Nancy to a hockey game. In the middle of the game, she turned to me and said, "Just out of curiosity, what do you tell people when they ask about us and our relationship?"

Relationship! Oh no, there was that word. Even worse, there was that question that was never supposed to be asked. The question I never wanted to ask myself, never-mind answer. There was no place I could run or hide. It was time to quickly think outside of the box. I simply pretended I had not heard the question and commented how loud it was in the arena. She immediately let the question go, and I had dodged another bullet. After all, I had a strict rule, and I wasn't about to break it.

However, I had one other problem. God really didn't care about my rule. God had a plan, and he was not about to let me get in the way of it. I now know why all the apartments I had chosen were mysteriously taken when I went to rent them, and why only one apartment was left in the one place I never would have chosen for myself.

As I walked her to the door after the hockey game, I reached down, grabbed her hand, and thanked her for the nice night. She just looked up at me, and somehow I couldn't look anywhere else. I kissed her. It felt almost perfect and wonderful. Then I opened my eyes wide and realized I had broken my rule! How could I break my cardinal rule? I was now dating my best friend. I never saw it coming. What happened to the cool, disciplined guy who was always in control? For better or worse, I was now in a relationship. Who would have seen this coming? After all, I was an FBI agent! I was trained to think ten steps ahead, or so they kept telling us at Quantico.

I wanted our new relationship to have a chance; therefore, I knew I had to move to a new location so we wouldn't be next door

Daniel J. Williams

neighbors anymore. I had been thinking of building a new home for some time. Now I was ready.

When I moved Nancy and my sister, Mary, who had moved to Louisiana earlier, were there to help me decorate, pick out wall colors and purchase the furniture I needed. Nancy was in her element. I think she viewed this as a safari adventure. This is when I learned about her love of shopping, especially when it involved my money.

Since both of us wanted this relationship to work, we took a commitment to never go outside the boundaries God had established for unmarried relationships. Therefore, we agreed not to let the physical boundaries already established between us change.

In February 2001, Nancy and I were married. Sam acted as my best man. During his customary toast, he said, "When Dan first introduced me to Nancy, he introduced her as his friend. A few months later, whenever I asked him if anything was developing between them since I often saw them together, Dan would just say, 'We are friends.' Over the course of the next year, I asked him the same question several times, and I always got the same reply. So Dan, the question I have for you tonight is, are you still only friends?" Leave it to my good buddy to start a roast rather than a toast.

Nancy and I officially a couple.

The Memories to Come

I couldn't help but smile as the memories of our life together flooded my mind as I laid there in bed gazing at the ceiling. She was still my best friend after all these years, and soon, through God's grace, she would be the mother of our child. And on that thought, I started to drift asleep.

The next day, Nancy and I got up to go to work. We both were infused with excitement at the thought we would soon be parents. Both of us were confident this was God's will since we believed he had placed it on our hearts. God was always faithful, and we were sure it would be just a short time before the laughter of our baby would fill our house. Before I left the house for work, I peeked into the room that would soon be our baby's. I could just imagine all the days and nights that would play out in this room.

CHAPTER 3

The Supporting Cast

I was now working the type of investigations I enjoyed the most — criminal cases. I had served in many places with the FBI including Baltimore, Mobile, New York City, New Orleans and several times in Washington. But my assignment here in Oklahoma City was my favorite. More importantly, I didn't have to prepare to battle with the top brass like I did at FBIHQ. As I pulled into the parking lot, I had no idea how important a role this great group of people would play out in my life over the course of the next seven years.

In Oklahoma City I had the opportunity to lead some of the finest FBI personnel in my career. They were all homerun hitters. This included three of the best criminal racketeering agents in the FBI. SA Gary Johnson juggled a myriad of responsibilities to include being our media coordinator and my Principal Relief Supervisor. He had a knack for building great cases. There were few agents out there who possessed his ability to sweet talk even the toughest criminals into a confession. Gary was simply one of the nicest agents you could meet.

SA Todd Keck was a West Point graduate and U.S. Army ranger. He had an unbelievable work ethic. He was relentless and extremely smart. He could turn a lump of coal into a diamond. He also had

26

The Miracle of Kayla

a sharp wit that was quick to jump on any miscue someone made, especially if that someone was me.

I once had a supervisor tell me I was the finest agent on his squad, but I was also the biggest pain in the neck at the same time. (I'm actually paraphrasing where he thought I was a pain.) He prayed every night I would step into management and be blessed (or cursed) with having an agent just like me to supervise. Well, his prayer came true. I had SA Clayton Simmonds. He was extremely hard-working, tenacious, dedicated, smart and capable of making some of our best cases.

Clay loved to give me his opinion on just about everything, especially if I had no control over whatever he was complaining about. He would come into my office almost daily and give me his laundry list of what he thought needed to be changed in the FBI.

Adding to my headaches were the numerous times Clay and his co-conspirator, Todd, would come barging into my office unannounced. The two of them took pleasure in torturing me daily. I often asked them why they couldn't be nice like Gary, but I quickly learned to stop that because it would just add fuel to the fire.

Todd had a knack for getting Clay all spun up. In a split second the tables would turn, and Clay would get Todd all worked up. The two of them would feed off of each other, and I would have to deal with the perpetual flame of grief that would fan out in my direction. The daily back-and-forth, which would often go on throughout the entire day, was something I strangely relished in.

Eventually, I established a little wooden doghouse in my office. I had little cardboard characters representing each agent. When any one of them messed up, they would put themselves in the doghouse until they demonstrated proper remission for whatever mistake they created. It was all meant in good humor. I also intended to dish out a little humility; however, that idea went right out the window when it suddenly was viewed as a badge of honor to be in the doghouse.

Both Clay and Todd seemed to be permanent residents in the doghouse. Somehow the two of them managed to highjack my doghouse. Suddenly, everyone was in the doghouse including me and Sam who was now in Oklahoma City. I had used that old dog house effectively for years, and within less than one month, they took what was humorously meant to be a Hall of Shame and turned it into a Hall of Fame.

Yet, I wouldn't trade any one of them for ten agents. We played hard together, often at each other's expense, but we always had each other's back. It was a great feeling knowing I was in charge of a group of highly skilled people that I could depend on.

Tommy Terhune after a seizure of 16 pounds of methamphetamine.

I also had the great pleasure of forming a task force with the Oklahoma City Police Department (OCPD) to target gangs and criminal enterprises in the area. The officers of the OCPD and their Special Projects Unit were clearly some of the most professional,

The Miracle of Kayla

dedicated officers I ever had the pleasure of working with. I specifically had the honor of partnering with Lieutenant Tommy Terhune. He was their Special Projects leader, SWAT Team leader, and general encyclopedia of just about every criminal in the area.

No matter how early I came to work or what time I left, Tommy was still on the job. I honestly thought he never went home. Yet, he still made it a point to get in his daily workout.

More importantly, we both shared the same mindset and strategy when it came to investigations. We believed investigations that had the deepest impact were long term, strategically driven cases that employed comprehensive methods such as wiretaps and undercover operations. Neither of us were for picking off low hanging fruit and calling it a day.

During my tenure in this position, our squad and task force worked numerous investigations resulting in the arrest of nearly a thousand of the state's most dangerous, violent felons. We were never bored from a lack of work. Every day was something new — bank robberies, kidnappings, drugs, gangs, hostage situations, child pornography, child prostitution, money laundering, and a host of other federal violations. We were even recognized for investigative excellence by the national Federal Law Enforcement Officers Association, as well as numerous other awards.

As I walked down the hallway to my office this day, these were the last cast of characters I could have ever imagined playing such an important role in the events to unfold. Yet it is the least likely characters that God uses to tell his stories. He weaves the tapestry of our lives with the people he places in it.

And so Nancy and I embarked upon our new journey to start our family. Together, we prayed God would equip us and make us ready to be his surrogates. We placed our faith and trust in his divine plan.

Front Row: SA Dawn Woody, SA Todd Keck, SA Andy Kerstetter, SA Mitch Holmes, SA Doug Frost, SA Paul Ladner, SSA Daniel Williams, Melissa Shawver, Kim Weems, SA Doug Samuels, SA Doug Goodwater. Back Row: SA Casey Cox, Det Phil Williams, Det Josh Herren, SA Clay Simmonds, SA Gary Johnson, Det Scott Smith, Det Tobias Frederick, Det Jae Kang.

CHAPTER 4

The Unexpected Detour

We started our journey confident that God would bless our lives soon with the laughter and turmoil that comes from having a newborn baby. Nancy and I were certain this was his will for our lives. He had after all placed this dream in our hearts, and he was always faithful. Each night we talked and planned for the child who would soon occupy our lives.

Suddenly our weeks turned into months and our months into years. Every month we would find ourselves waiting with anticipation to see if Nancy was pregnant. Each month we were greeted with disappointment when the pregnancy test came back negative. We would then start praying again that God would bless us with a child the next month.

Yet our prayers went unanswered. Adding to our frustration were the constant inquiries from people who would innocently ask us when we were going to start a family. As the years ambled through, we began to think there was something physically wrong with us. Subsequently, we sought out a medical opinion.

We learned while I was capable of having children, time was now working against Nancy. She was in her mid-thirties, and her chances of getting pregnant were growing slimmer. While a man normally produces sperm most of his life, a woman is born with all

Daniel J. Williams

the eggs she will ever have. Once she starts to menstruate, she loses eggs each month that will never be replaced. When she approaches her mid-thirties, she usually has a small number of eggs left capable of reproduction.

The physician discussed with us the latest medical advances ranging from intrauterine insemination (IUI) to in vitro fertilization (IVF). Both were expensive, particularly IVF, and rarely covered by insurance, especially in Oklahoma. Both were very intrusive and required precise timing. Both involved the risk of multiple births. IVF involved the use of expensive drugs administered through painful shots several times per day over the course of many weeks. It was followed by a surgical procedure to extract the eggs and to fertilize them with sperm in a Petri dish. If the eggs were fertilized, which was not a guarantee, then they had to be surgically returned to the uterus several days later. The price of each IVF procedure could range as high as $20,000. This had to be paid out-of-pocket upfront regardless of whether or not it was successful. Needless to say, I learned more about the female reproductive system than I ever wanted to know.

I could tell the years of trying to conceive were weighing on Nancy. We had some lengthy discussions about our next step: infertility treatment or adoption. She was beginning to struggle with the notion she was possibly barren. Infertility, at least for Nancy, connoted a sense of defeat and frustration. She was saddened that she could not become pregnant, particularly when those around her were all having children.

Somehow, she felt she had failed me as a wife. It was the furthest thing from the truth. I loved her regardless of whether she could conceive or not. Yet, there were days the thought of being barren became very difficult for her, and I would catch her crying. Often times her frustration was directed at me, and I found myself at a loss on how to comfort her. I would hold her and let her know she was all I needed. However, I am not sure how much solace it brought her.

We initially started to talk at length about adoption. We tried

The Miracle of Kayla

to research as much as we could. We later learned of an all-day seminar that we decided to attend. They had sessions on domestic adoption, international adoption, adoption law, and numerous other topics. We went to every session we could fit in. The average price for adoptions ranged from $17,000 to $25,000. One of the downsides was the wait time. Depending on the type of adoption you pursued, wait times could range from a year to several years. Yet both of us were beginning to get excited about the prospect of adoption. At lunch time. we wondered out loud if God was leading us in this direction.

Also present at the seminar were several adoption agencies from around the state. After lunch, we stopped to talk with as many as we could and to gather numerous brochures. However, to our surprise, each of them had an age cut-off ranging from forty to fifty. I was now over the cut-off age for most agencies. This really struck both of us as unfair. I was in better shape and more physically active than most people in their twenties. Yet, despite all we had to offer a child, each agency advised we would not even be considered if one of us was over the age limit. When we inquired about the reason for such a policy, many could not articulate a solid reason. Some would not even offer a reason.

One agency opined that birth mothers were less likely to choose adoptive parents in their forties. Therefore, the agency did not want to waste couples' time and effort trying to place a child with someone in that age range. She also said it was not fair to take a prospective couple's money on a slim hope of realizing their dream of having a child. While I disagreed with her, I respected her honesty. However, I thought that should be a decision the prospective adoptive couple should weigh.

The age limits set by some agencies seemed arbitrary to me. It missed the mark on all we had to offer a child to include financial security. It was my understanding the home study was to weigh the suitability of the individual couple and not to discriminate them

33

Daniel J. Williams

based on an age restriction. However, you could not have a home study if you were not eligible.

Needless to say, we were both disappointed when we left the adoption seminar. Neither of us could understand how there were so many children out there who needed a loving home, but a couple who had so much love and numerous other advantages would be disqualified for something as arbitrary as an age limit. Both of us were in excellent health, well educated, had respected careers, financially set, and I even had the luxury of being eligible to retire with a great pension in several years. Yet, we were unable to adopt because I was simply too old, even though I was really in the prime of my life. Now I felt as if I had let Nancy down. We would not be able to adopt because of me. Now it was her trying to comfort me.

I could have looked at the prospect of using an attorney to facilitate an adoption, but the truth was I did not trust many attorneys. I had been in law enforcement too long, and I had heard all the intelligence reports of unscrupulous attorneys who engaged in unethical practices when it came to adoptions. I knew I was tainted by all I heard. I fought hard not to have my bias be an indictment on an entire profession.

I subsequently contacted several attorneys I respected, but they were not involved in adoptions. They really didn't know any specific person they could or would recommend to me. I even had several caution me to do a complete, thorough investigation of any attorney I chose. They advised attorneys tended to be more expensive, and in some cases, the practices used by some were questionable.

I contacted several federal and state prosecutors who were close friends of mine. While none of them were knowledgeable of any good adoption attorneys, they cautioned me as well. Several attorneys told me they thought I would have better luck using a professional adoption agency because they were probably more capable of caring for the birth mother, prospective couples seeking adoption, and more importantly, the welfare of the child. Nevertheless, I wasn't sure if I could overcome the age requirements of some of the agencies.

The Miracle of Kayla

While I was far from contacting every agency, it was becoming clear this was an avenue that God did not seem to want us to venture. At least that's what I initially believed, even though it didn't make a lot of sense to us. Needless to say, we were greatly disappointed. Yet, we were both sure it was God's will we would one day have a child. Surely he would not have placed this strong desire on our hearts only to endure one disappointment after another. It appeared our options were running out. Therefore, we decided it was time to further explore how medical advancements in the area of infertility could possibly help us.

We then scheduled an appointment with one of the leading infertility physicians in the area. This was a man who was highly respected in the medical community. However, what we liked the most about him was he was very empathetic towards our problem, and he took the time to listen to our story. He wanted to spend a good deal of time learning about us and our desire to have a child. I also think he wanted to make sure we were committed to the road we were about to travel. He explained our various options, the positives and negatives of each, the expense, and the likelihood of success that was clearly not on our side due to Nancy's age. We knew from our initial consultation we were in good hands even if we were unsuccessful.

After a great deal of consultation between Nancy and me, we informed him we were ready to try. We then filled out a lot of paperwork to start the process. Each of us inhaled deeply and set our hearts and minds on the new course we were about to chart.

The Medical Route

As part of the process, we had to complete a medical history. Years before I met Nancy, she had undergone a surgery to remove a large ovarian cyst. After we underwent a medical examination, the doctor discovered mild endometriosis and suspected scar tissue

Daniel J. Williams

from Nancy's prior surgery might be contributing to her inability to conceive.

After consultation, the doctor commented that surgery to correct these issues might help. Nancy, a medical professional herself, understood there was always a chance of scar tissue forming after any surgery. She even suspected she had scarring because of the occasional abdominal pain she felt. Therefore, together we agreed to first try surgery consisting of lysis of adhesions and vaporization of endometriosis. This was medical terminology that I had little knowledge about. I just understood it might be an explanation for why we were unable to conceive.

What Nancy and I understood was the doctor wanted to start with the most conservative approach. Yet, he was very clear this might be just one of many possibilities why we were having difficulty trying to conceive. The surgery appeared to be successful, but we understood it might not be the panacea we desired. He then told us to keep trying as we had previously.

Once again, disappointment seemed to greet us each month. The following year, another decision was made to remove an endometrial polyp that had formed. Again we were told to keep trying, but to no avail. Time was clearly running out.

This was followed by a decision to start oral fertility medicine, which was not covered by insurance. Before we realized it, we had gone through four cycles of treatment without any success.

We were now ready to move on to the next step. The doctor recommended we start with the less intrusive and least expensive procedure of IUI with oral fertility medicine. While it was less expensive, it was anything but cheap. Nevertheless, we waited with anticipation to see if it worked. Once again, a sense of dismay seemed to overcome us when we learned Nancy didn't get pregnant.

Yet undeterred, we knew God was not going to let us down. Therefore, we decided to try again. We subsequently tried three more times over the course of the next year. Now a sense of despair hung over us like a cloud.

The Constant Reminders

The drugs were starting to affect Nancy. Her whole hormonal balance was off. She was very emotional, moody, and would quickly become agitated. Often it was directed at me for no reason at all. It was clear she and I just needed time to collect our thoughts before we could make another move forward. It was becoming even more apparent to me this was taking its toll on Nancy. There was little I could do to alleviate her sense of failure. Yet, it was also taking its toll on me. I thought a little time without trying would do us both good.

Still, the stress kept extracting its price on Nancy. Mother's Day was always difficult. While she was happy for the women who got to celebrate this day, it always served as a reminder of the void in her own life. Yet she would smile and pretend. While I applauded the church for recognizing such an important day, I wished they would have remembered women who were struggling with infertility. Father's Day wasn't much better for me.

One day we were sitting in church when a young couple sat in front of us with their newborn infant. The child was beautiful and all dolled-out. Suddenly, it was too much for Nancy to handle. She got up and ran out the door. I knew why. I got up and found my wife weeping. There was nothing to say. I just held her and led her out the church.

On another occasion while sitting in church, a family with four young children got up in front of the church to dedicate their newborn. They were a beautiful family. All I could think of was how fortunate and blessed they were. They seemed to have everything I wanted. When I turned to look at Nancy, I could see her eyes watering up. I knew how difficult this was for her. Would we ever get to share in such a dream? Would we ever have the opportunity to dedicate our own child to the Lord? I just held her hand tightly. It was the only thing I could do to let her know she wasn't alone in her pain.

Sometimes it seemed God was taunting us rather than helping

Daniel J. Williams

us. It was clear Satan seemed to be attacking us from every direction. I could only pray God would help us to remain faithful to the dream we believed he had placed on our hearts. Doubt was now creeping into my mind. It seemed easier to forgo the dream and just walk away. "Surely if it was God's will, then it wouldn't be this hard," I often wonder out-loud.

The time came when Nancy could no longer go to any baby showers. She would always send a card and a gift, but the thought of attending was too much for her to handle. She once confided that she was so disappointed with herself for feeling jealous of women who could conceive with such ease.

I knew she was going through a difficult time. Yet, I had so little to offer that would bring her any measure of comfort. I too was frustrated and weary by the years of trying to conceive in vain, but it would be dishonest to say I could fully identify with the burden she was carrying.

We continued to throw ourselves into our work. If anything, it served as an escape mechanism for each of us. However, there were times when my job would take me places that served to remind me of how unfair life could be.

One day, Clay obtained a search warrant to look through a house occupied by a woman maintaining drugs for a local gang. After we entered the premises, we discovered she had several children in addition to a cache of drugs. I decided to move the kids to another room while Clay and Gary attempted to obtain a confession from the subject. I guessed they ranged from the ages of six to nine years of age. Each had different fathers who were incarcerated at one time or another. One child even showed me a letter she carried from her father. The letter was addressed from the state penitentiary. It was more focused on what he wanted the little girl to tell her mother to bring during her next visit. There was little interest expressed about the little girl.

Weeks later, we conducted a major gang arrest. When we entered the house of the main subject and his girlfriend, we found several children in addition to guns and drugs. As the task force was

The Miracle of Kayla

searching and interviewing the subjects, the children were segregated in another room. They were inquisitive about the weapons the officers carried. They would then describe the types of weapons they would select when they played their video games. All I could think of was what type of world was this where the topic of discussion for a young child was the best weapon to use.

A few months after this, we would target another very violent gang. The gang had a history of gun and drug violence. During our investigation, we repeatedly learned about impending drive-by shootings. We were constantly having to stay several steps ahead to prevent every violent act they were going to commit. The leader of the gang was a man who had a long criminal history. He had been recently released from jail for a violent offense. After his release, he quickly reestablished his position as the gang's leader.

One day a woman approached the gang leader, who had fathered her child prior to his incarceration. Her boy was now a teenager. She pled with the father to leave their son alone. The boy was a good student and star athlete. He had a chance to make a good life if his father would just break off all ties with him.

Despite all the possibilities that awaited the young man, he was enamored with his father's lifestyle of drugs, guns, fast cars, women, and power. Therefore, his father recruited his son into the gang. This included the ritual known as "jumped in." It is the moment a potential gang member gets beaten-up simultaneously by every member of the gang. If he survives without running away, he is officially inducted into the gang. It symbolizes the motto of "blood in, blood out." It was just another way of saying the only way out of the gang is through death.

I could only shake my head in disgust. I could feel the grief and pain of this poor woman trying to save her son from a life of crime. Yet, she could only sit by helplessly as the man who spent nearly a decade in jail led their son into the gang life. What kind of father could jump his own son into a gang? Unfortunately, I was anesthetized to it by now.

Daniel J. Williams

During my career, I would estimate nearly ninety-five percent of the criminals I arrested came from broken homes where the father was either absent, unknown, incarcerated, or abusive. Many were left totally unsupervised. Drugs and alcohol were just a way of life. Sadly, the only resemblance of family was found in the gang life.

All this served to remind me of the family Nancy and I were so desperately trying to have but couldn't. We had so much love to give. Where was God? Why was he not helping? It didn't seem fair that criminals who could care less about children seemed to have no problem having as many as they could. Yet we couldn't even have one child. I felt guilty thinking such a thought. While it was a thought born out of jealousy, it was also derived for a genuine concern about the kind of lives these children would have to face.

After a little time, Nancy and I had a chance to take a deep breath. We were still convinced this was God's will. We were ready to take the next step.

The Next Step

IVF is not a quick or easy procedure. The truth is it takes a lot of preparation and time, as well as money. Many people often don't have this as an option because it is so cost prohibitive. Plus, it does not guarantee success and can also be painful, both physically and emotionally.

At one point, Nancy questioned if IVF was too sterile. "If God wanted us to have a child," she inquired, "wouldn't he just allow it to happen naturally?"

She wasn't alone in her thinking. I too shared the same sentiment. There was little doubt in my mind other people struggled with this same thought. In addition, IFV initially posed a moral dilemma for me. I was concerned this method might be a way of man playing the role of God.

However, I reasoned even the best of science was not going to

The Miracle of Kayla

help if it wasn't God's will in the first place. I opined if an embryo was formed, even outside the womb, it was a child in God's eyes. Either way the embryo still has to be embedded into the womb to survive. This is what we were doing. Yet, even an embryo inside the womb is not guaranteed to grow to full term unless it is God's will, no matter how it got there. There are millions of children conceived through IVF. Are their lives considered any less human? No. They were conceived through the hand of God. This reasoning ended any moral dilemma I might have possessed.

I assured Nancy God allowed this technology to be developed by the hands of men to add to his heavenly kingdom. The trained physicians who performed the technique, were mere instruments of God's mighty hand. This brought her the comfort she needed to proceed to the next step.

We were now ready to take this next step. While I had complete faith God wanted us to have a child, I began to convince myself God helps those who help themselves. Since I was fairly sure he was not going to intervene in the same manner he did with Abraham and Sarah, it was easy to convince myself this was the only door left open for us. Subsequently, we went into the finance office and paid the whole amount up front. The thought of writing the check for such a large amount with no guarantee of success was a little hard to swallow. Therefore, in 2009 we prepared ourselves for what we knew was going to be a tough and difficult road.

Precision was the key to success. We had to make everything come together so Nancy would produce the greatest number of viable eggs possible. Even then, we knew it would not be many. This involved the injection of numerous shots every day to stimulate the development of healthy follicles. Nancy began injecting herself several times a day in the abdomen.

Later, she would need a progesterone shot every day. This was the part of the process that required me to administer the shot since it had to be given in the upper, outer-quadrant of the hip muscle. The thought of giving her a shot with a large needle sent chills up my spine. It also didn't help that these shots were an oil-based solution that took even longer to administer and were quite painful.

I was reluctant about telling her I had never given anyone a shot before. I figured she had enough stress already without adding that tidbit of knowledge to her anxiety level. Therefore, I secretly sought out help to learn how to deliver the shot. Over two dozen oranges bear the scars of my medical education. When the time came for me to administer the first dose, I was literally shaking. I tried to joke around to make her feel at ease and to calm my own nerves.

This went on day after day. Yet as painful and tedious as it was, Nancy marched on like a true soldier. I couldn't help but admire her strength, courage and determination. How I loved this woman. Somehow our struggle had brought us even closer. I never believed we could be any closer.

As expected, the medication came with the side effects that the doctor had told us about. Nancy suffered from nausea, abdominal welts, and hot flashes. In addition, she often suffered from severe mood swings. I confess this was not an easy time for me either. I never knew if I was going to be met by either Dr. Jekyll or Mrs. Hyde from one minute to the next.

Still, I knew all of this created an enormous amount of stress for her because she felt like so much was riding on her shoulders. I tried to ease her load by letting her know I was there to bear the burden with her. It was also in God's capable hands. We just needed to trust him. While I know I brought her some comfort at times, she still couldn't shake the belief she was responsible for the outcome, even though she knew in her heart God was ultimately in control.

On top of the gruesome shots were the intrusive transvaginal ultrasounds. These were used to examine the ovaries. Then she would have blood samples taken to check hormone levels. It made me glad I was a guy and not a woman. I now understood why my gender was truly the weaker sex.

When the time was right, she was brought in to undergo a minor surgical procedure. She was unconscious during the procedure in

The Miracle of Kayla

which they used ultrasound imaging to harvest eggs through the pelvic cavity. They were only able to retrieve three eggs. After the eggs were married up with sperm in a laboratory dish to stimulate fertilization, they were monitored for several days in the laboratory to observe the outcome of the fertilization process. If they successfully fertilized, they would call us to return so the newly formed embryos could be surgically transferred back into Nancy's uterus.

After the egg removal, there wasn't anything Nancy and I could do. Those next few days seemed to pass by so slowly. I couldn't seem to do anything long enough to make time pass by quickly. We had to be ready to go anytime, on any day of the week, so that Nancy could be escorted to the surgical room to transfer any successfully developed embryo(s).

A few days later they called. We got to the clinic in what seemed like a few minutes. After we arrived, the doctor advised us they only had two embryos. He wanted to make sure we understood the risks of multiple births, and the procedure could still be unsuccessful if they failed to implanted within the uterine wall. We told him we clearly understood the risk. I was asked to leave while the nurse escorted Nancy to the surgery room. She then underwent another minor surgery to transfer the embryos. When she regained consciousness again, the doctor told us we could go home and relax. Relax! He had to be joking. He said he would have us come back in a week to take a blood test to determine if we were successful.

Now we were again in a waiting mode for the next week. Neither of us wanted to talk about the possible outcome. We seemed to be afraid we would jinx everything. However, prior to leaving the hospital, we both agreed despite all the money we had spent, and the best of medical assistance, God was still the one who would decide if he would bless us with a child. Then I led us in prayer, and it was now in God's hands.

43

CHAPTER 5

A Prayer Answered

Approximately a week later, we were summoned to the doctor's office, where Nancy was given a blood test. We were then told to come back in an hour to learn of our results.

It seemed like the longest hour of our lives. Both of us tried to prepare ourselves should the results come back negative, and we wondered out loud what we would do if that were the case. Would we try again? Were we ready for another ordeal? Were we ready to fork out another large sum of money for what might be a wing and a prayer? Was it really God's will we have a child, or were we just masquerading our desire for his will? Somehow during that hour, it seemed easy to talk about the negative. The positive seemed too fleeting to embrace.

After the hour passed, we walked back upstairs to the doctor's office prepared for the worst. The first thing we noticed was the doctor and his staff were waiting for us. *Oh no, what did this mean?* Together, we just held each other's hand tightly.

When we walked over to them, the doctor said they had just received the results. He smiled and said, "Congratulations, you are going to have a baby." The news we had waited so long to hear. I was simply at a loss as to what to say. Nancy broke down sobbing, and I immediately reached out and held her in my arms. Everyone

44

The Miracle of Kayla

was coming up and hugging us. We were having a baby! God had delivered on his promise after five years. He was indeed faithful.

After nearly thirty minutes of continuous congratulations from various people, we started to walk to our car in the parking garage. Actually, we seemed to float on a cloud on the way. Neither of us could let go of the other.

After the tears stopped, the realization we were about to be parents was setting in. We just sat in the car holding each other's hand. Finally, we felt the freedom to dream about our family. It was as if the dark shadows were driven from the room. The first thing we wanted to do was praise God for the wonderful gift. We instinctively knew this baby was his child, and we were given the honor of being his surrogates.

Naturally, the next thing we wanted to decide was how long we should wait to tell everyone. We knew we had a lot of people praying for us. Nevertheless, we decided we should wait until after the third month had passed just to make sure the pregnancy was viable. Both of us agreed we would remain firm on this position. We then drove home so Nancy could get her car to go to work.

On the way to the office, I figured it really wouldn't be a violation of our newly established covenant if I called my close friend Michael Roach, a retired OCPD major, who was the U.S. Marshal for our district. Mike had been appointed by President George W. Bush. He had many responsibilities as the marshal, one of which was to command the fugitive task force in our district. I had locked arms with him early on by designating one of my finest agents, Doug Frost — a great investigator with a remarkable ability to hunt down fugitives — to participate in his task force. Mike and I were just great friends who could talk to each other about anything. He was one of the few people I confided in about all the trials and tribulations we were experiencing trying to have a child. Our friendship also had a mischievous side.

On one occasion, we were invited to a formal dinner to listen to Governor Jeb Bush speak about education. Oklahoma Governor

45

Mary Fallin introduced him to all of us. At one point I had to leave the room to take a call. When I returned to my seat, Mike said, "Stand up quick! The governor wants to recognize any FBI agents at the dinner." Without thinking, I stood up. Suddenly the crowd started to clap. I confess for one brief moment I felt very important. That was until my wife grabbed my hand and told me to sit down. Apparently, the governor was trying to recognize the few people who put this affair together. When I looked at Mike he was almost on the floor laughing.

I knew he was a devoted Christian who was praying for us. Therefore, I called and told him the good news. He was elated for us. In fact, he actually got all choked up because he knew how much we wanted this. This was the kind of friend Mike was.

U.S. Marshal Mike Roach.

Then somehow I deceived myself into believing it wouldn't be a violation of the firm rule Nancy and I had set an hour earlier if I notified my family. Naturally, it wasn't a violation if I also told my best man at our wedding. Sam was ready to tell everyone, but I swore him to silence because I had taken an oath of silence (omertà). Therefore, he was committed to the same oath of silence.

The Miracle of Kayla

When I arrived in my office, I earnestly tried to remain true to my earlier pledge. However, this lasted about two minutes when the whole squad wandered into my office. They could tell by my step something was up. Besides, they were trained investigators. Just about every day, they heard me tell them they had the privilege of studying under the foot of the master. Therefore, the master couldn't be upset if they noticed something different. Subsequently, I reasoned I could not be held responsible for the outstanding investigators they had become. The truth was I was so excited about this new blessing, I had to tell the world. I guess it didn't say much for maintaining secrets in a secret organization!

Later when Nancy returned home, she sheepishly blurted out her confession of how she failed to keep the pledge and had told just about everyone. I of course professed disbelief and indignation she would trample on such a sacred pledge. I informed her she had violated our omertà, and I reminded her of the penalty if she was a member of the mafia. She gave me a half-hearted "sorry". I smiled and then informed her that I too had violated our oath and told just about the whole world. Now, I could overlook her blabbing, but me … I'm in the business of secrets. But when God blesses your life, it is hard to remain silent. You want to tell anyone with ears who will listen how great God is.

The next several weeks were exciting. We would go out to dinner and spend hours talking about possible names if the child was a boy or girl. We talked about the type of upbringing we wanted for this child, including education, college, discipline and most of all, the need to raise this child to know Jesus. We would go to furniture stores and baby stores looking at cribs, bedroom sets, and clothing. We wanted so much for this child. While we did not know the child's gender, nor had we yet met, we were so in love with this person who had already blessed our lives.

Life seemed like a whirlwind of window shopping and imagining how the baby's room would look. I started to research everything I could get my hands on concerning raising a child. I even found

Daniel J. Williams

myself downloading information on changing diapers, feeding babies, and learning the art of how to swaddle infants. I am sure I wore out most of my squad. I was constantly seeking their advice on child rearing as often as I was inquiring about the status of their cases. My life was beginning to take on a new meaning other than the FBI. Already this unborn child had stolen my heart.

Nancy was continually going for her prenatal checkups. I was usually there with her. But one day, after the doctor did his check up, I could see he had a look of concern. Before he said anything, I tried to prepare myself for any disheartening news. He turned to Nancy and said, "I don't want to alarm you, but I am only hearing a faint heartbeat. It could be anything, to include the position of the fetus. We just need to wait a few days. I believe we could hear a stronger heartbeat then."

Tears of worry started to appear in her eyes. I immediately smothered her hand with both of mine. My heart was pounding with anxiety, but I had to pretend an air of confidence so I could ease her mind. The problem was I was having trouble trying to maintain my own composure.

When we left the office, she just threw her arms around me and started to sob. I wanted to join her, but I knew I had to remain strong. Surely God would protect our child. After all, it really was God's baby. We were just his surrogates. We then sat in her car and prayed. God was good. He was our only hope. He would not forsake us.

On the way back to work, I prayed out loud. It seemed at times I was trying to negotiate with God. "God, you are always faithful to your word. In John 15:7 you said, 'If you remain in me and my words remain in you, ask whatever you wish, and it will be done for you.' God, I have tried so hard to follow the dream of raising a child that you placed on my heart. Yet I feel you have placed us on a roller coaster ride. I'm not sure how much longer my wife can hold out. I'm not sure how much longer I can hold out. Please Lord, remain true to your word."

The Miracle of Kayla

When I finished, I sounded like I was trying to blackmail God with his own word. The thought of losing our child and the pain it would cause Nancy was too much for me to bear. In all candor, I was more frightened by this prospect than I was when the New York SWAT team, of which I was a member, burst into a bomb factory manned by armed terrorists intent on blowing up parts of New York City on June 3, 1993.

Suddenly, despite badgering God, a blissful peace came over me before I arrived at the office. It seemed to reassure me God was in control. His will and timing, no matter what, were perfect. I just needed to keep my faith in him.

CHAPTER 6

God's Will

The next several days were extremely difficult and stressful. We each threw ourselves into our work. My squad was up on several wiretaps. We were juggling a wide variety of violent crime cases ranging from bank robberies to kidnappings. But Nancy was never far away from my heart and mind.

Nancy told me early one morning she was going in for another check-up. I told her I would call and clear my calendar, but she insisted that I didn't. She wanted to go this time by herself. While I was extremely reluctant about letting her go alone, I somehow knew my presence was not going to ease her anxiety. She reassured me that she felt this would be a routine check-up and that everything would be fine. Somehow I didn't believe her, but I wasn't about to argue with her.

While I tried to stay busy in the office, I mostly paced back and forth from one squad to the next. I tried to engage people in substantive conversations, but I could barely focus. My usual sarcastic demeanor and ability to clown around had disappeared. My mind was with Nancy. I couldn't concentrate on anything else. I could only wait for a call from her to learn the fate of our child. I was totally frustrated and helpless. The day just passed by so slowly.

Later in the afternoon, I decided to use the FBI gym to work

The Miracle of Kayla

out. I was hoping to take my mind off of Nancy's visit to the doctor. Besides, I was of little value in the office. No matter what I did, I just couldn't focus. Another friend, Supervisory Special Agent (SSA) Charles Spencer was already in the gym when I arrived. Unfortunately, he had to spend most of our workout session listening to me rambling on about government inefficiency. It was my way of venting my frustration and angst onto something else. He was just kindly lending his ear as a sounding board.

About twenty minutes into the workout, my cell phone rang. For one brief second I was almost afraid to answer it. Nevertheless, I ran for the phone as if my life depended on it. When I picked up and said, "hello," there was dead silence on the phone.

"Nancy, are you all right?" I would repeat my request several times, but the silence was deafening. I could tell she was trying to gather herself to speak, but all I could hear was a faint whimper. Finally, she started to cry.

"Nancy, please, please, tell me what is going on," I demanded.

Then came the words I dreaded, "I lost the baby."

Now I was silent. It was as if a dark cloud had just cast its shadow over me. I had to be there to help her through this tragic loss. But what possible words of comfort could I provide. All I could spit out was, "I am so sorry." I couldn't get anything else past the lump in my throat. I just wanted to hang the phone up so I could grieve and express my anger with God.

After a few minutes of silence, I said, "Stay where you are, and I will come there to pick you up and take you home, sweetheart."

In a barely audible voice she muttered, "I will just meet you there. I need some time by myself."

"Take as much time as you need. I will be at home waiting for you." Before I could say another word, she hung up.

I just sat there on the bench unable to fathom why God could let this happen. I was heartbroken. This child my wife carried was more than just a fetus or a glob of tissue. It was my child, my heart and soul. Although I had never met him/her, I loved this baby more than

51

Daniel J. Williams

my own life. Everything I had I would have gladly forsaken. I could only sit there thinking about all the dreams we had that were now gone … the child I would never meet, the smile I would never see, the laughter I would never hear, and the hug I would never embrace. My mind raced through all the life events that would never be, such as birth, the first day of school, prom, college, a wedding, and grandchildren. I could feel the tears in my eyes beginning to form.

Spence could see I was upset. He got up and walked over, placing his hand on my shoulder, and inquired if everything was all right. How I appreciated his kindness. Yet it took everything I could muster just to voice the word, "Yes".

He tried to pressure me for more, but the lump in my throat would not let me utter another word. I had to leave the office, so I just got up and walked away silently.

In the car heading home, I found myself yelling at God. "How could you allow this to happen? How could you place a dream on our heart, and then let us fall after we spent all these years trying to obey your desire? What kind of God would inspire a dream in us, then place us on a roller coaster of hope and despair? Where is your love? Where is the God who walks beside his chosen to keep them from falling into a pit of despair?"

I couldn't believe I was yelling at God. Why was I still alive to utter another word? Who was I to challenge God? I was just a wicked, wretched sinner! I just cried out for his forgiveness. "Lord, forgive me. You are my God. Nothing is impossible for you. Your will is perfect. Please God, just help me to understand. Help me to be the man you need me to be for my wife who is grieving. I am at a loss to even explain this or to offer any words of comfort. I don't even have any words of comfort for me. I am not even sure I know how to properly grieve this loss or to help Nancy through her grief. Lord, forgive this simple, stupid man."

I remember the prayer well. In my life I have come to learn, often the hard way, the Holy Spirit speaks to your heart and leads you only when you humble yourself before God.

52

The Miracle of Kayla

Suddenly, my soul felt comforted by a feeling that overwhelmed my heart saying, "Your child is my child. He was from the moment I created him. I have taken him home to be with me where he will never know suffering and pain, only complete and eternal joy. One day, you will meet your child. He will know you, and although you were not able to give him a name, you will know him by the name I gave him. You will hear his laughter, caress his face, and know his joy. You will feel his embrace when he thanks you for your faithfulness. I did not create him to live only months in his mother's womb. I created him for all of eternity."

Wow! Was this the Holy Spirit speaking to me or a compilation of every sermon or scripture I had ever read? It happened in just an instant! It wasn't drawn out like some conversation or even statement. It was more like someone took a sledge hammer and imprinted it on my soul. An imprint that was so clear it left no room for misunderstanding. The FBI agent in me wanted to fully examine what just happened. I guess it was my curse. I wanted to over-analyze everything. Yet, how can you investigate the unexplainable. Was it the Holy Spirit? Maybe, maybe not. I couldn't prove it, but in my heart I wanted to believe it could be even though the rational side of me was willing to dismiss it as my subconscious mind desperately searching for an answer I did not have. Whatever it was, it brought me the peace and understanding I needed at that moment. It was the only thing that mattered.

In just a short car ride, I was given my answer. It wasn't what history would record as a burning bush moment, but then again, I wasn't called to lead God's people out of Egypt. I was just inspired to heal the heart of a woman who was hurting and blaming herself for the loss of our child. It was all I asked and more. And yes, in that short car ride, the possibility that I might have had a child who graced heaven seemed like a great reason to celebrate rather than to mourn. A child who I love to this day, though we have never met.

When Nancy got home, I could tell she had been crying. I just put my arms around her and held her as tightly as I could. I suggested

Daniel J. Williams

we just go for a walk around the lake and neighborhood. During our walk, I told her about my conversation with God, to include the part where I yelled at him. I also told her about the message I felt was placed on my heart. I hoped it would be the message she would let God place on hers. She just placed her head on my shoulder, and we walked without saying a word. Together, we spent the next hour in silence mourning our child and the special moments that would never come. Our child was with our heavenly Father now. In our deepest sorrow, this thought brought us peace and comfort.

CHAPTER 7

One More Try

The next few months seemed like a fog at times, but we still had not given up our faith and hope in God. How blessed we were to have our Sunday school who continued to pray for us on a daily basis. The power of their prayer continued to sustain us each day afterwards. I also gave thanks to God for my good friend, Mike Roach. He was not only praying for us, but he was always there to let me bend his ear. He always had words of encouragement. When I told him what I believed the Holy Spirit placed on my heart, he got choked up. God had placed this faithful man in my life for a reason.

When the time was right, we sat down again to chart our next course of action. What do we do now? Do we try IVF again? Do we shell out all that money after we just learned first-hand that science was no guarantee? Was Nancy ready and willing to endure all the physical pain again?

We talked for several hours. We weighed the pros and cons, but the one thing we were sure of was God wanted us to have a baby. Our situation certainly did not make it impossible for God to bless us. The Bible was filled with stories of people just like us who were unlikely to have a child, but God was faithful and delivered. I just wanted him to tell us how to proceed, but the answer never seemed forthcoming.

Daniel J. Williams

Adoption seemed clearly out of the picture; therefore, we both agreed we needed to take one more attempt at IVF.

We later met with the doctor who advised he would try a slightly different protocol concerning the procedure. He thought it might enhance our chances. While all that was nice, we knew it wasn't about him, us, or any new twist on the procedure. It was simply about God's will. His will was sufficient no matter what the outcome was. God would provide because he was always faithful. How he would do it was the question we didn't have the answer to.

We had to wait a short while in order for Nancy's body to recover her hormonal balance. When she was ready, we inhaled, paid our money upfront and placed it in God's capable hands.

The procedure was about the same except that Nancy was required to take higher doses of the medicine, which took its toll on Nancy's body again. We were still stressed. Nevertheless, we plowed through it firm in our faith.

After Nancy underwent the surgeries to transfer the only two embryos they could retrieve, all we could do was sit back and wait. It was still nerve racking. Time was running out for us now, and we knew it. Nancy was forty, and the chance of success was not in our favor. Yet we were ready for this new fight.

When I was young and competing in the ring, we would often travel to different gyms to spar with other opponents. It was good to get out of your own stable of fighters to compete with other fighters in order to hone your skills. In many of the gyms, I often saw an old boxing platitude near the ring that read, "It is not the size of a man in a fight that matters, but the size of the fight in the man." It was a knockoff of something Mark Twain had allegedly said about the fight in a dog, but like so many other sayings, he probably never uttered the words. Yet those words always resonated with me. It spoke to me about determination, perseverance, and a steadfastness to strive on when you had nothing to physically give anymore. Simply put, it spoke to me of courage in the face of adversity.

As we were leaving the hospital, I could see how this simple

The Miracle of Kayla

platitude was so descriptive of my wife. Although she had a small frame, she had as much fight in her as any heavyweight champ. She had been through so much, but she was still ready to continue the fight. There was no surrender in her. Knocked down and teary-eyed at times, she would wipe away the tears and get back up in defiance of her adversary. Although she had never been in the ring in her life, she knew God was in her corner. No matter if she lost the round, she was never going to throw in the towel because she could rest on her faith in God.

The time came for Nancy to take her blood test to determine if she was pregnant. We sat patiently in the hospital cafeteria waiting to return. We tried to talk about anything but the possible results. Instead, we conversed about things going on with her job and our respective families. Alas, the time came to return upstairs.

When we got there, both of us noticed something wasn't the same as the last time. This time there was no doctor or group of people, only the nurse. She asked if we would follow her to her office. I knew this was not going to be good tidings. She then broke the news that the procedure had been unsuccessful. While I was filled with regret, I could see the tears streaming down Nancy's eyes. She had undergone so much. While I was always by her side, she was the one who had to endure it. I reached out for her hand. The nurse kindly tried to offer words of comfort and condolence. We thanked her and walked out the office.

We were both silent on the way home. There was little to say. We both understood this was the will of God, but that didn't bring us a great deal of comfort. It was what it was, and we couldn't change it. She just stared out the window into the distance without saying a word.

The next several weeks we both walked around in a daze, seeming to just go through the motions. It was difficult to admit to people the procedure didn't work. Our Sunday school class tried to offer comfort. Nevertheless, it was always hard to answer people when they would well-meaningly inquire how our efforts to have a

Daniel J. Williams

child were progressing. Sometimes all we could do was smile and thank them for asking. Then we would just walk away. But the truth was we just needed a little time.

One night we decided to go to a hibachi grill. After seating us, the waitress then sat a couple with an infant in a carrier nearby. The baby was absolutely beautiful. Suddenly, Nancy got up and ran to the door. I quickly followed her. Once outside, she buried her head into my chest. I had no words to offer her except to hold her.

She cried out, "It is not fair that we can't get pregnant when we have so much love to give. I feel like I let you down."

I just continued to hold her. I wanted to say something that would ease her pain, but I didn't want to say anything that would minimize what she was feeling. Her pain was real, and there wasn't anything I could say that would change that fact. I too shared a similar torment.

Several weeks later while eating out, Nancy looked up from her plate and inquired if we should give IVF a third try. I had thought hard and prayed about it a lot during this time. I must have asked God about it every day. What did he want us to do? How did he want us to proceed? Yet, God seemed silent. I could only conclude from his silence, it was not how he wanted us to proceed. Perhaps for now, he wanted us to do nothing. I confess that for an assertive personality like mine, this answer was hard to accept. I was used to fixing things. This is what I do. I am the fixer.

Yet, I think God was trying to tell me something through his silence. His plan was not something I was ever meant to fix. He did not need me to fix or tweak anything he had already set in motion. He created an entire universe very well without my help. All he wanted from us was our faith and obedience. He had this, and I just needed to trust him. At the same time, I did not want my wife to go through all that emotional and physical pain again. I told her it was time for us to step off this roller coaster ride. God would show us in his time, but for now we had to wait.

Her eyes were glassy, but she knew it as well. Although I am not

The Miracle of Kayla

a woman, I could only imagine how difficult it was for Nancy to finally come to the realization her womb was closed. It was as if she was coming to the point where she had to say goodbye to this one part of her life to move forward. I'm not sure how much men can fully grasp this innate desire to bring forth life, or the loss of self-worth when you realize your time has come and gone. I'm not sure this is true for every woman. There are many couples who choose not to have a child, and I nor anyone else have the right to question that choice. All I could do was be there. It seemed so little when I was so use to fixing things. But there was nothing I could fix. I was engulfed with a sense of helplessness.

CHAPTER 8

Getting off the Canvas

When I was young, I spent a good part of my life in the boxing ring. The life of a fighter brought forth many metaphors that seem fitting for many different circumstances in life. My trainer, Lou Desmarais, would bellow them out at me constantly, whether I was in the ring sparring or hitting the heavy bag.

Lou, a former Marine Corps veteran of the Korean War, had become like a second father to me. Whenever I would start to tire out from the hard training routine, he would push me to dig down deep. I could hear his mantra, "You are never out of the fight until the final bell rings," echo in my head, even when I was training alone.

During one fight, I got knocked to the canvas late in the first round after taking a hard right cross to the chin. I had dropped my left hand and stepped into my opponent's right cross. After getting back up, the bell rang. I was discouraged because I was doing so well until that moment. I still had two rounds to go, but I felt like I had let my corner team down. Lou was there waiting for me and sensed my discouragement. I knew before I got to my chair, he would have some encouraging words. Yet he motioned to the rest of the corner to remove my stool.

When I staggered back to the corner, he physically lifted my chin up. "Good," he said as he pulled out my mouth piece.

60

The Miracle of Kayla

"Good?" I protested. "I just kissed the canvas!"

"Good because you got back up. Good because you now know you have heart, and now your opponent knows it too."

I looked across the ring at my opponent who looked like he was doing just fine. Based upon my observation, it looked like he was just having another leisurely day at the office. "I'm not too sure he agrees with you. He looks like he is ready to finish me off and call it a day."

"Even better," as he placed the cold compress on my head. "He is going to come out overconfident, but trust me, deep down he knows you got heart."

As I looked across the ring, I wasn't sure my opponent had received Lou's message. Actually, he looked more like a hungry lion, and I was the raw meat.

"Now get back out there and keep that right hand up as you pepper him with that great left jab. When the time is right, let go of that mean left hook of yours to his midsection. Then we will find out how much heart he has. I know you are a champ. Now make him believe it as well."

After standing the entire minute in the corner with Lou, who would not let me sit down, I was all pumped up for the second round. He believed in me, and now I did too. My confidence was restored. I came out for the second round making full use of the ring as I kept sticking him with the left jab. In the third round, I caught him with a solid left hook to his midsection after I ducked his right cross. He buckled, and I seized the moment landing one punch after another until the referee waived me off.

I would often joke with Lou that I thought he had seen one too many boxing movies. Yet he always knew how to motivate me. Many times I just wanted to win the fight for him. Lou's affirmation meant more than many of the trophies I would take home. Later in my life when I would train young fighters, I often drew from my friendship with Lou and the lessons he taught me.

Now, after the loss of our child and all we had been through, I felt as if I had been hit with a hard right cross and had been dropped

Daniel J. Williams

to the canvas. I wasn't sure if I could get back up. I wasn't sure if I wanted to. Yet I knew I had to find a way to pick myself up to continue the fight. Any success I had in the ring came not from the fact I was faster or stronger than my opponent, but from the fact I had heart and could usually stick to my game plan. I had the ability to view it as a chess game. Often I had to out-think my opponent by several steps. It was time to use these old clichés in my life to get motivated again. I just didn't know where to begin!

Now I realized I was in a different fight. Only it seemed my opponent — time —had me way outclassed. In my mind I was now in the realm of impossibility. It was like being in a fifteen-round championship fight with only seconds left on the clock after I had already lost every prior round.

I was simply feeling sorry for myself. I knew it, but it was so easy to do! My father's admonition of "thinking outside the box" seemed too trite and inappropriate for what we were going through. I could have easily gone on perceiving myself as a victim, until another memory flooded my mind.

"You are only a victim if you chose to be a victim," my dad would say as he was chewing me out for whatever new offense I committed that was surely going to lead to my inevitable grounding. It was a speech I would hear all too often during my youth. "Life is too short to live your life as a victim. Victory goes to the man who is willing to stand up, brush himself off and get back into the fight. Now you can sit there pouting on your bottom, in which case I will give you something to pout about, or you can stand up like a man and tackle the problem facing you."

I assumed he thought he was talking to a sailor under his command instead of the young boy I was. Yet, he was not about to let me make excuses and feel sorry for myself. He was right, and I knew it. After all these years, his value system was still dictating my life. As a young boy, the things he would often say went in one ear and out the other. Now they were constantly resonating and hitting me over the head decades later. I knew I had to get back off the canvas and continue the fight.

I was finally getting it into my thick skull I was not in control of this fight. I needed a good corner to go to, and I needed one fast. What better corner to go to than God's! It was the one place I watched my father go time after time. I remember falling on my knees in church the next Sunday. God had planted this desire in my heart, and I was still waiting for my burning bush moment. Surely, he would reveal his plan to me. I prayed as powerfully as I could. Nevertheless, no answer seemed forthcoming.

Although Nancy was throwing herself into her job to keep busy, I could tell she was antsy. I think she was still trying to find meaning to her ordeal, while simultaneously trying to hold onto any nugget of hope she could. I wanted her to know I was never going to give up. We believed deeply God had a plan for us. Together, through him, we would find a way. Somehow, I think she drew strength from my confidence in God.

So now it was my turn to carry the football, and there was no way to do that without God's help. I kept asking for some sign, but none seemed forthcoming. I had to remain content with simply waiting on God. One day as I was reading God's word, I came upon Isaiah 40:31, "but those who hope in the Lord will renew their strength. They will soar on wings like eagles; they will run and not grow weary, they will walk and not be faint." I guess this was a clear reminder that I was to wait on God.

Yet, I would foolishly ponder if God understood my makeup and my desire to jump into things head first and lead the charge. *What a foolish question* I would later think. Of course God understands my nature. He is the one who formed me in my mother's womb and made me who I am. Who I am, what I feel, and what I do come as no surprise to him. Nevertheless, I just needed a sign he had not forsaken me.

Somehow I found a file of old adoption pamphlets we had obtained at the seminar we attended years earlier. There was nothing

Daniel J. Williams

new. We were still ineligible because of my age. However, something moved me to check out other agencies online. I called several of them, only to find out they too had the same age restrictions. I was getting nowhere. Finally, I called a place known at the time as Heritage Family Services, which would years later merge with Nightlight Christian Adoptions. After I called, they graciously sent us some information. However, they too had an age restriction. I remember the let down and flippantly commenting to God this was another empty hole.

Nancy was still struggling with the miscarriage and second failed IVF attempt, so I didn't want her to know I was investigating adoption opportunities again. She had led the efforts with the infertility procedures, so I decided to spearhead the adoption option.

I continued my search to no avail. Several weeks later, I entered my home office to find I had left the information from Heritage on the top of my desk. Suddenly I heard this little voice inside my head say, "Call again." While it seemed frivolous, I called and spoke directly to one of the agency directors, Debbie Nomura. We talked for almost an hour. I told her as much as I could about Nancy and me. She kindly listened intently to every word. She told me I was welcome to fill out the initial paperwork. However, she didn't provide a lot of hope that they would deviate much from their age requirements. Once again, another dead end I thought.

I filled out the paperwork and sent it to Heritage, but I had little hope this would ever be a viable option. Therefore, I set about the task of calling every agency I could dial. Each time I would say a prayer before I called. I was met with the same obstacle at every turn. I had so much love and opportunities to offer a child, as did my wife. I had done things in my life other men could only dream about. But somehow I couldn't get around this age thing. Now it was I who felt I was letting Nancy down. No matter what, it was an impossible stone I could not move.

A few days later, I came into my home office. I saw the pamphlet from Heritage sitting on top of my desk. *I thought I threw this away.*

The Miracle of Kayla

Once again, I heard that little voice inside my head say, "Call again." So I called Debbie to plead my case one more time. She was anything but encouraging.

It seemed by now I had called every adoption agency, but I was getting nowhere. It was downright discouraging, and I was running out of patience. But I had not heard the final bell, so I was determined to continue the fight.

Several days later, I walked into my FBI office and again found Debbie Nomura's phone number and pamphlet on my desk. *How did this end up on my work-desk?* I never brought it into the FBI office to the best of my recollection. I was sure I had thrown it away with the rest of the documents at home. Why would I even want to bring it to work? Yet, there it was.

I had tried to plead my case earlier to no avail, so why was this agency's number and brochure still popping up everywhere when I thought I threw it away. As I was about to throw it away, I once again heard that little voice in my head say, "Call again. This time think outside of the box." Okay, somewhat different this time. But "think outside the box?" Where did that come from? How many times did I hear my father say those same words? I was out of ideas. How was I supposed to do that? Nevertheless, as I once again got ready to place the call, I prayed to God and asked him to intervene. I asked him to provide me with something, anything that would help me "think outside the box" and change their policy.

I have no doubt poor Debbie wanted to avoid talking with this crazed man who just couldn't seem to take 'no' for an answer. Again, I spent a great deal of time going over all we had to offer a child. More importantly, I told her about the love we had to offer. She said she would have to talk with her husband, Mike Nomura, the president of the agency, about this situation. She still didn't seem optimistic. Suddenly, I asked her if they would at least consider averaging our ages. Nancy was approximately twelve years younger than me. Averaging our ages would put us well below the age restriction. She said she would bring it up to Mike. *Where did*

65

Daniel J. Williams

I get this idea? It was truly "thinking outside the box," but would it make a difference?

I was left with a feeling that if anyone had the ability to modify the age limits, it was the Nomura's. They had a real passion for bringing children and adoptive parents together. They believed it was God's calling for them. It was also clear they truly loved their job. You could feel the love in their hearts for children, birth parents and couples seeking adoption. Mike was even completing his law degree because he wanted to build and strengthen his nonprofit agency. It was the best I could hope for. I knew they would be fair and give it thoughtful consideration. I was content to place it in their capable hands, no matter what their final decision was.

In the meantime, I still had not told Nancy anything about what I had been trying to do. I couldn't bear to see her get hurt again by having her hopes elevated, only to see them snatched away at the last minute. Nevertheless, I was determined I would find a way. I would not let her down. We had always been open to adoption until we learned of the arbitrary age restrictions. In our eyes, an adopted child was the same as a biological child. We understood what a gift an adopted child was because we clearly understood each of us were adopted into God's family through the grace of Jesus Christ.

The next day I was driving to a meeting when Debbie called me. I held my breath as I pulled the car over so I could talk.

"Mike and I spent a lot of time talking about your situation. We also prayed about this. We made the decision to average your ages. Therefore, you are eligible to proceed with the adoption process through us."

Hallelujah! I could not stop thanking her enough. When I hung up the phone, I could not stop thanking God. Clearly, he was the architect behind this decision.

At the end of the day, I could not wait to tell Nancy. How was she going to react since I never told her what I was trying to do? At first she looked at me with disbelief. She wondered if this could be possible after all the previous doors had shut. When the truth began

The Miracle of Kayla

to sink in, she was thrilled that God had opened a door that up until now had appeared closed.

We started to pull together all the required documents. There was so much to do! We had to gather a plethora of information just to complete the paperwork. We each had to write an autobiography about ourselves and produce numerous reference letters. We were fortunate to have so many respected people write letters on our behalf to include my friends Mike Roach, Sam Macaluso and the leader of our Sunday school, John Butchee. Clay Simmonds also wrote a wonderful letter.

We also had to have our fingerprints taken for the background checks. While I have fingerprinted numerous subjects, I only had my fingerprints rolled when I applied for the FBI and the military. I had forgotten what it felt like to have my prints taken. We would later go through a thorough home study and personal assessment.

We also had to develop a life book to present to potential birth parents. This would provide them with information and pictures of us. This was one of the most difficult things to do. It felt like you were revealing everything about yourself with the hopes someone might find you interesting enough to keep reading. It was like being a puppy on display hoping someone would choose you. And just because you initiated the process, that didn't guarantee you would be chosen. Nevertheless, we were absolutely elated God had opened a new window and were content to just place our trust in him.

I had been asking for a sign for so long. God had placed it right there for me to see all the time, but I overlooked it because it was too simple. I was looking for the waters to part and the sky to burst open so God could miraculously reveal his wonderful plan. He simply placed an adoption agency brochure right there in front of me. He even placed it on my heart what he expected me to do. Apparently, he had to do it four times before I understood this was the sign I had been searching for. How often have I missed the miraculous signs in front of me because I was searching for the burning bush.

67

Mike and Debbie Nomura.

CHAPTER 9

"Mariah"

Like IVF, adoption comes with risk. Not only were you putting up a substantial amount of money, you were also putting your heart out there for potential disappointment.

Adoption laws are rightfully designed to protect the birth parents, especially the birth mother. Many of these women are often vulnerable and alone. Many have no place to turn for help. Their decision to place a child for adoption is weighed very heavily, but ultimately, they chose to seek what is best for their unborn child. I cannot imagine the gravity of having to make such a momentous decision. The depth of such love and sacrifice has always touched Nancy and me. The thought someone would entrust us with such a gift was an overwhelming honor.

After completing a successful home study, we were now eligible to be selected by birth parents. It was now a waiting game. We were anxiously hoping to be chosen as adoptive parents.

Approximately eight months later, we got a call from Debbie. A woman who was over twelve weeks pregnant was seeking to place her unborn child for adoption. She had gone through all the available life books of prospective couples praying to adopt a child. During her review, she chose us. She was interested in meeting us.

By adoption practice, all Debbie would tell us was her name was

Daniel J. Williams

Mariah. She was having a girl, she had gotten pregnant after a one-night stand, and the father could not be located yet. However, he was probably living out west somewhere. He might have been employed by a cellphone tower company that took him on the road often. Mariah had provided Debbie's agency with the ultrasound and blood work. However, she had no real income and was in financial need to help provide a roof over her head and other miscellaneous items. The court had already granted authority for financial support. In addition, Mariah had several other children that she could barely support. She and her children had talked about placing this child up for adoption. They mutually agreed this was the right thing for all concerned.

She wanted to meet us. Wow, could it be true? Was this really happening? We could not meet her soon enough!

Debbie arranged for us to meet Mariah at a local restaurant in February 2011. We arrived first and waited in the entry area. When they approached the door, I could clearly see Mariah was beginning to show. We introduced ourselves and sat down at the table. She appeared to be shy and uncomfortable, but Debbie, who was an expert at these things, knew just how to jump start the conversation.

We engaged in small talk initially until the meal arrived. But as time progressed, our conversations became more substantive. Mariah clearly knew I was an FBI supervisor and Nancy was a pharmacist and college professor. After discussing ourselves, we then got to learn more about her.

She had a tough life. She was approximately forty-one years old. She was carrying a baby girl, and was due on or about May 11, 2011. She also warned us that her previous pregnancies went past their due dates. She expected to deliver the baby in Norman, Oklahoma. We learned the name of her doctor. The baby appeared to be in excellent health. She did not have the financial means to care for and raise another child, but she was against abortion. Instead, she had decided to give this child up for adoption. It made her feel better knowing the child would have opportunities she did not. She confessed she

The Miracle of Kayla

did not know or remember the name of the father. She did, however, remember his birthdate was in August 1967 because she liked to know people's astrological signs.

I confess I had to fight the FBI agent in me from rearing its ugly head. I have an instinct developed over years with the bureau to know when someone is lying or withholding information from me. I was also very good at getting to the truth and obtaining a confession from some of the most hardened criminals. This was one of those times when my antenna started to go up. I had a hard time believing she did not know this guy's name. Surely most people know at least the first name of the person they are sleeping with rather than just their astrological sign. If it had been only she and I having this conversation, I would have pressed her hard for more information.

But desperation has a way of bridling your instincts. I realized this lunch was more about her interviewing us than it was about us interviewing her. How she got pregnant didn't matter to us. She was about to give away the most precious gift, and we were hoping she would select us. Therefore, we continued to talk. Before our conversation ended, I had her laughing.

Nancy and I later got in the car and talked on the way home. I told her about some of my concerns, yet they seemed ordinary for a woman who was alone and afraid. People don't want to immediately open up to someone they barely know, especially if they feel they are being judged. I surely wouldn't. At least this is what I convinced myself. Nancy had reviewed the ultrasound and blood test briefly and said they looked good. Both of us felt God was leading us in this direction. We needed to trust and follow him no matter where he led us. Now we could only hope we were what she was looking for to raise her child.

The next day, Debbie called to say Mariah wanted us to be the adoptive parents. We were both elated. We were going to be parents at last. Debbie advised the court had authorized us to pay her necessary living expenses during her pregnancy, which were slightly over a $1,000 per month. She also warned us they would still have to

71

Daniel J. Williams

locate the father to get his permission, or at least demonstrate to the court every reasonable attempt was being made to locate him. I was briefly tempted to ask her to give me just a little information about him, and I would find him in a short time. I also knew she couldn't do that, so I bridled my desire to ask. She also wanted to remind us again that the birthmother had the right to back out at any time prior to terminating her parental rights in court. Nancy and I were aware of those risks but were willing to take them. We felt strongly God was leading us, and we needed to be obedient to his calling.

May seemed right around the corner, and we had much to do in the following months. We wanted to share our joy with everyone. We were going to have a baby! Time could not go by fast enough.

We kept in touch with Debbie who was keeping us updated on Mariah's progress. Mariah reported her pregnancy was progressing well, and she was still intent on the adoption. We continued to pay her monthly expenses, as well as the fees to the adoption agency.

Nancy and I had so much to discuss such as names, schools, child care, college, and baby furniture. There was no subject we didn't cover.

A month before the due date, we went out and bought baby furniture, baby clothes, baby toys, nursery music, and a baby mobile to hang over the crib. We enjoyed every moment. This is saying a lot because I absolutely hate to shop. I shop like a hunter. I go in to get what I need, bag it, and carry it home. I don't even take the time to look at anything else. But Nancy was in her element. She was a pro and loved shopping. I loved just watching her enjoy herself. She had been through so much. It was great to see her return to her former jovial self.

May 11th was fast approaching. Debbie called one day to inform us Mariah was told by her doctor she would have a later delivery date than anticipated. She reminded us that Mariah had previously gone past her due dates, so we weren't too concerned.

The new due date was just a few days away when Debbie called to advise us Mariah was told by her doctor he was going to induce

The Miracle of Kayla

labor on May 26th if she had not delivered by then. We were still concerned, but trusted her doctor knew what he was doing.

The nursery was now ready, and we were prepared for the blessing God was going to deliver to us. I would often peek inside the baby's room just to imagine how our lives would change. On Sunday night, May 22nd, I saw Nancy standing by the door stealing a glance inside the room. Even from behind, she looked angelic. I walked up behind her and put my arms around her. She laid her head on my right shoulder as she placed her right hand on my arms causing me to squeeze even tighter.

"Dan, do you ever wonder how much our lives will change in the next week?"

"Sweetheart, there is not a day that goes by when I don't pass by this room and stop to imagine the moments that will take place in here."

"I can see the many days and nights we will spend in the room. I can see her wrapping her daddy around her little finger. What a wonderful father you will be!"

"How lucky our daughter will be to have such a magnificent mother like you. I will be so blessed to have both of you in my life!"

And for the next fifteen minutes, we just stood there with my arms tightly wrapped around her, and her head just resting comfortably on my shoulder. Nothing else was said. Nothing else needed to be said. In that moment, we were locked together as one emotionally and spiritually. We could see the future that awaited us. A future we would share with our daughter from the first moment we would place her into this crib. In those fifteen minutes, we could see our baby's life unfold before our eyes. It was a vision I had often seen play out in my mind as I recalled the memory of my own father spinning my sister in the air. Now, through the faithfulness of a loving God, I too was less than a week away from realizing my long-awaited dream of being a dad.

The next day while I was at work in my office, SA Mitch Holmes, a member of my squad, came in and placed a note on my desk. I held

Daniel J. Williams

Mitch in high esteem. He was a tremendous athlete who had played baseball prior to entering the FBI. He and I would often talk about sports. He was forever pitching me quotes from famous baseball players, especially catchers.

I often used him to train my new agents. I had also placed Mitch in charge of most of our violent crime programs. He had a real passion for children and eagerly sought out to be our division's crimes against children coordinator. I knew he would always be there to answer the bell when we had something involving a child. I cannot count how many times I would call him at 2 a.m. to check on something. He would immediately leave his house to run it down even if it turned out to be nothing.

However, when he handed me the note, he said, "Boss, I don't want to cause you any concern with all you are going through, but I thought you should see this. I just received this information."

I thanked him and started reading it. It concerned adoption frauds that were taking place across the state and the large number of people who were being scammed. It sent shivers up my spine. Much of it sounded like the things we could be going through. I placed it on my desk and closed my eyes. Surely, I had nothing to fear. God was in control. He would not allow such a thing to happen. I decided this was something I did not need to share with Nancy.

The following day, I reached out to Debbie to ask her to update me. Debbie had been trying to contact Mariah without any success. She planned on traveling to the Oklahoma City area to meet with Mariah at her apartment or hospital on May 26th. Her voice didn't seem reassuring.

On the morning of May 25th, Nancy asked me if there were any updates on Mariah. I told her about my phone call earlier with Debbie, and how she was having trouble contacting Mariah. I tried to reassure her we would hear something soon, but I wasn't very convincing. What I did not tell her about was the information I received earlier from Mitch.

Later that evening, unbeknownst to me at the time, Nancy was

74

The Miracle of Kayla

beginning to have an ominous premonition that something was wrong. Before she left work, she slipped into the hospital chapel to pray. As the tears began to fall from her cheeks, she pled with God to keep Mariah and the baby safe. Yet, in her heart, she could see her dream slipping away.

CHAPTER 10

May 26, 2011

The big day had arrived. Neither of us knew what to do. Should we wait at home or go to work to kill time until Debbie called us? Since there wasn't anything we could do concerning Mariah's delivery until Debbie called, we decided to go to work.

After a short while in the office, Detective Phil Williams of the OCPD came into my office to talk. Phil was an old-school cop who had keen investigative instincts. He had been a member of our Safe Streets Gang Task Force since its inception. When he got his hands onto a case, he would follow it relentlessly to its final conclusion. He also had a reputation for not being afraid to rock the boat, which did not always endear himself to upper management. Phil was never afraid to give you his opinion, even when you didn't ask for it. People with a thin skin were often offended by his direct comments. I always enjoyed the banter between us. He would inevitably say something that would leave me in stitches laughing. But more importantly, he was my friend.

But this day we just sat and shot the bull for a while. He sensed I was anxious, and when he asked if there was anything wrong, I told him we were waiting to hear from Debbie concerning the delivery. But I also told him about the information that Mitch had given me and how it had caused me a little concern. I said I was probably

The Miracle of Kayla

making more out of it than I should. Before leaving, he advised me he was going to be on the south-side of town. If I needed anything, I was to call him immediately.

Now I was getting nervous. It was midmorning, and I had not heard anything yet. The information Mitch provided me days earlier was starting to resonate with me. Suddenly, I started thinking about all the worst case scenarios. Why had we not heard anything yet? I had to put these concerns out of my mind. I called Debbie for an update. She was on her way to check on Mariah at the hospital. If she was not there, she was going to check on her at her residence.

Debbie had not heard from Mariah in several days, nor was Mariah answering any of Debbie's calls. Debbie was getting worried but promised to call me once she had any news. Now I was worried. My mind started to race. The report started to weigh even more heavily on my mind. This was beginning to unfold like the scenarios in the report.

Furthermore, some very bad storms had recently swept through like they always seem to do in May. Could Mariah have been hurt in the storm? I was getting desperate. My mind was searching for any possible answer. I had a gut feeling that was telling me something I did not want to believe.

No matter what my mind seemed to conjure, it would inevitably drift back to the worst case scenario. This sometimes seems to be the curse of being an FBI agent. What did I really know about this woman? I didn't even know her last name or where she lived. I could not even check to see if she had a criminal record. Even though I was sure the agency had checked her out, they too would not have found a criminal record if she had provided a false name. However, the FBI had an arsenal of ways to discover someone's true identity. But the worst thing I could imagine was the impact to Nancy if this was a fraud. If it was, it was all my fault for not listening to instincts that had been highly trained by the best law enforcement agency in the world. All I could do was trust in God and place it in his capable hands.

Daniel J. Williams

While waiting, Nancy called. *She was the last person I wanted to speak to right then.* I feared the conversation we might be having at the end of the day. A conversation I was simply not prepared for.

"Danny, have you heard anything yet?"

"Debbie is on her way to the hospital. She said she will call us when she learns something. I am sure everything will be all right," I lied. I wasn't sure who I was trying to convince, her or me. My instinct was now telling me something different. I knew this situation was going bad quickly. I could only wait and let it all unfold before I could act. Beating myself up would have to wait. "I'll call you as soon as I hear anything."

When I hung up with her, I just started pacing the building. I would casually stop and talk with people in the halls or at their desks. Yet, when I would walk away, I couldn't remember what we talked about. My mind was clearly somewhere else.

Soon I was back at my desk fielding calls from FBIHQ and other law enforcement agencies. I was just beginning to get hungry. Deciding where I wanted to eat was the biggest decision I was prepared to make at that moment; however, Sam needed me to provide him with some gang statistics. It was the one thing I could do in my sleep. I knew every gang, their composition, affiliation, membership numbers in every part of the state, and the scope of every investigation we had targeting them. Providing this information to Sam took my attention off of everything else my mind was vying with at that instant.

After giving him with the information, I started to get ready to head out the door for lunch when the phone rang. It was Debbie. I could tell she was upset. I initially had a difficult time hearing a word she was saying. Finally, I gathered that Debbie had just been chased away from Mariah's residence by a large man when she went there to check on her.

Suddenly, my FBI cap was back on my head. I told her she had to provide me with Mariah's full name and address. She might have been hurt by this guy or worse. I assured her that police officers

The Miracle of Kayla

would conduct a welfare check on Mariah's status immediately once Debbie gave me the information. She willingly complied. I knew Debbie was emotionally upset and overwhelmed by the incident. She informed me she was going to return to the hospital with the hope she might have missed Mariah previously.

Reliable Phil! He had just told me where he would be, and Mariah's address was on the south side of town. Somehow Phil had a knack for being at the right place at the right time. Phil possessed a demeanor to get to the bottom of something quickly. If this guy was in the process of hurting anyone, Phil would find out.

I also reached out to SA Casey Cox from our office. Casey was a young agent who had just arrived from the Baltimore Division. He had a beautiful family, and it was easy to tell they were his number one priority. I garnered from our conversations he was a devout Christian. Casey was a graduate of the Air Force Academy prior to his career with the FBI. More Importantly, he was an outstanding investigator and would turn over every rock to make a case. I had watched him numerous times turn a lump of coal into a diamond simply because he would not quit. He was like a pit bull when he bit into a case. He would not let something go until he had run every possibility to the ground. Besides being extremely diligent, Casey was a skilled interviewer. Therefore, once he had arrived in the Oklahoma City Division, he was like a race horse ready to run as soon as the gate opened. He was the type of agent to whom you could assign a task and know in your mind you could consider it done well before you ever walked away.

Casey and Mitch set out to the address planning to meet up with Phil. I knew all three of them would get the answers we needed. I called Phil back to inform him they were on the way.

In the meantime, I thought about returning to my house to see if I had any additional information on Mariah that could help the investigators. I called Debbie back to tell her law enforcement officers had been dispatched to Mariah's residence. They would quickly get to the bottom of this matter.

79

Daniel J. Williams

Before I could leave for the house, my phone rang again. It was Nancy. Oh no, what was I going to tell her? While I was consumed with trying to learn the status of Mariah, Nancy was foremost in my mind. I couldn't bare the heartache it would cause her if this whole drama was a fraud. Was there anything I could say that would ease her mind? Should I hold off on alarming her or prepare her for the worst? I realized at this point, there was nothing I could say or do. I had to tell her we were unsure of Mariah's status.

"Have you heard anything yet," she asked. I then told her about Debbie's ordeal, but before I could finish she said, "I am heading to the hospital to meet Debbie. She might need my help. I'll call you when I get more information."

Great, my wife is now a detective, I thought to myself. Yet, I was relieved I could push back the dreaded conversation I feared.

The Call I Feared

Shortly thereafter, Phil called. He informed me the name of the guy who chased Debbie away was James Peters. (I have changed his true name and that of the other co-conspirator for reasons I will explain in the latter part of chapter 12.) Phil then hit me with news I did not want to hear. "Dan, I hate to tell you this, but there is no baby. There never was."

My heart sank. My worst case scenario had just come true! How would I ever explain this to Nancy? She had already been through so much. The thought of her heartache was cutting into my soul like a knife. Now I had to brace myself for the rest of the information Phil had gathered.

Phil continued to explain the details they had just uncovered in their investigation that revealed Peters had conspired with a woman named Claire Mitchell (true name changed) to fake her pregnancy. Mitchell, posing as "Mariah," would go to several adoption agencies to begin the process of placing her unborn child up for adoption. However, there was never a child. Peters and Mitchell had manufactured financial reports while simultaneously providing a fake ultrasound and blood work to several different adoption agencies. They would collect checks from the various adoption agencies, which were paying for her alleged living expenses.

After I hung up the phone with Phil, I was heartbroken. In one brief second, my world fell apart. The life I envisioned with our new baby was shattered. I felt as if someone had just stolen my baby and my life. I just collapsed back into my chair, placed my elbows on the table, and rested my chin in my hands. Yet I knew there was no time for grief. I now had to put my FBI hat back on, set my emotions aside, and do what I had been trained to do. There simply was no time to be a victim. The time to grieve would have to come later. The lesson my father taught me was now engrained into the fabric of my soul. It was time to get back into the fight. I had to get back home to find any additional evidence or information they might need.

Mitchell was not at her residence when Phil found Peters. Phil, Casey, and Mitch located her at a vocational school. They talked with her outside, and she eventually confessed. Later they brought her back to the residence where she consented to a search. Lt. Tommy Terhune sent other members of our task force to assist in the search. They discovered all sorts of documents and evidence. By the end of the day, they would be able to identify other potential victims across the country, including other adoption agencies that had been defrauded. Both Peters and Mitchell were subsequently arrested.

Mitchell knew who I was and what I did for a living. When we had previously met, she had even asked numerous questions about my work. What made her think she could commit a crime on a federal agent and get away with it? Had she become so arrogant from her previous success? Did she now think she was capable of successfully committing the scheme on anyone? If so, I knew I owed it to every victim prior to Nancy and me to ensure we would be their last victims.

Adoption fraud is often the unreported crime because the birth

Daniel J. Williams

mothers can change their mind at any time prior to terminating their parental rights in court. They can simply walk away without giving a reason. This was the loophole Mitchell could exploit that would prevent the unsuspecting adoption agency and couple from ever knowing there was never a baby in the first place.

Mitchell was willing to take the chance of defrauding an FBI agent, but it was a big gamble. A gamble she and several other people would lose. But unfortunately, so would we and every other potential victim out there. These other victims would also long for justice. I knew I was going to have to step up and be their advocate, even though I wanted to find a hole to crawl into.

Casey kept calling me with updates. How I appreciated his, Phil's, and Mitch's quick response. I knew I had placed the three best people on the case. I also knew there was still much to do. Yet, I knew they would do what was needed. I found comfort in that thought.

After I got home, Mike Roach called me. Mike had completed his term as the U.S. Marshal and was now the director of the unit in Oklahoma City responsible for drug interdiction. He was well connected and was a great focal point for law enforcement intelligence. He too was cognizant of the same information Mitch had given me. He said he would start contacting all his law enforcement sources. By the end of the day, we spoke several times. In addition to any information he could find, Mike was there to keep me from climbing the walls. He would prove many times that day to be a great source of comfort.

Nancy and Debbie had just arrived home. How was I going to tell my wife there was never a baby, and the dream we built our lives around was just a fraud? I could not bear to see the woman I loved have her hopes snatched away once again. I initially stood there petrified. She in turn gave me a mortified look. Now I had to present her with the news that was going to bring her to her knees.

Before I could start, she informed me what she had just learned. "When we did not find Mariah at the hospital, we drove to the

The Miracle of Kayla

doctor's office where Mariah claimed she was receiving prenatal care. At first the doctor was reluctant to talk to us in fear of violating the Health Insurance Portability and Accountability Act (HIPAA). I then showed him the paperwork. After reviewing it, he decided to speak. He immediately identified the blood results as a fraud. He saw that the patient account number and medical record number were short by one number. He also indicated that all of their reports contained both the patient's first and last name; whereas, this blood work only had the patient's last name. He had no such patient as a Mariah Petree."

Wow, my wife was thinking like an FBI agent; however, she rattled it off so fast, I could barely keep up with her. Unfortunately, I had not yet told her that Mariah was just an alias and that her real name was Mitchell. It was time for me to fill in the blanks and tell Nancy what we had just learned. However, I think she already knew this whole adoption was just a fraud. I could see the disappointment and fear in her eyes. I took a deep breath and said, "Nancy, there was never really a Mariah. It was just an alias she used to con us. The whole adoption was a fraud. A fraud they might have perpetrated on others as well."

I continued to tell her the whole story as she stared at me with a horrified look. A look I pray I will never see again. Her face was ghostly pale and she started to shiver despite the heat. I guess I had now confirmed her suspicion. It was the hardest thing I have ever had to do. Was God not done punishing me?

Nancy was devastated. She collapsed in the chair and started to cry. Through her tears she wondered out loud, "How could anyone do such a cruel thing? Why would anyone do something so horrible to hurt someone? They stole my baby!"

These were questions I had asked myself so many times during my career. The simple truth was there are no real answers other than the world is a cruel place, and evil people are everywhere. Even though this is not the answer that comforts a broken heart, it was all I had.

Daniel J. Williams

In our case, it was not so much about the theft of our money but the horrible feeling they had stolen our baby.

Out on My Feet

In that moment, I felt like I was being torn apart. One second I was trying to spearhead an investigation. The next I was trying to fathom a way to comfort my wife. In between, I was just hoping there would be time for me to crawl away in a hole so I could grieve. And then there was God! How could he have allowed this to happen? This was his fault, I reasoned. I was overcome with such anger at him, but this too would have to wait. I would deal with God later.

Suddenly, I was juggling a plethora of calls and trying to issue instructions, but the truth was it wasn't necessary. Casey, Phil, and Mitch knew exactly what do to without me telling them. Often before I could finish my instructions, they would reply, "We are already on it, Boss." They were already ten steps ahead without me dictating what needed to be done.

Yet, somehow remaining involved made me feel like I still had some measure of control. I guess I just needed to feel like I was still in the fight. I felt like I had just gotten hit with a hard right hook. I needed to get off the canvas and resume the fight. Instead, these three guys were taking up the fight for me. I could not ask for anyone better to initiate this investigation. I also found comfort in knowing that Tommy Terhune was coordinating other investigative steps on the ground by providing his resources and investigative experience.

Years earlier when I was still boxing as a young man, I would see fighters who, in boxing parlance, "were out on their feet." It was an expression to describe someone who was hit so hard they were technically unaware of what was going on but still fighting out of instinct. It happened once to me. I was hit so hard with a right hook I was knocked senseless, but I stayed on my feet, fighting out of instinct. I was fighting the way I had always been trained. My trainer

84

The Miracle of Kayla

later told me when I came back to the corner for the final round, I had a glazed-over look. I wasn't hearing any of his instructions. I just had this distant stare. I do not recall anything about that fight even to this day, except when they raised my hand in victory.

This is how I responded that day. I was working as an FBI agent at the same time I was trying to be a protective husband. It seemed at times I didn't know whether I was coming or going. I know I must have had that same glazed-over look I had years earlier when I returned to my corner of the ring.

Later Phil called to update me on the day. Their investigation was now focusing on whether or not Peters, Mitchell, and others were involved in a ring that conspired to commit adoption fraud in various states. One possible couple may have been defrauded several times and didn't even know they were victims yet. Peters and Mitchell were now in state custody, but a federal hold was going to be placed on them.

They were attempting to prey on couples like Nancy and me, who desperately sought to have a child to love. They were trying to steal from people by using a baby that never existed. But what they didn't realize or care about was the baby was as real for Nancy and me as any other baby out there. I have no doubt other couples would have said the same thing. It was almost as if they had stolen our own child because that is surely what it felt like.

While I understood adoption fraud was a risk, I also knew it was a relatively insignificant risk. The vast majority of adoptions took place daily without any such consequences. Unfortunately, this knowledge didn't ease my heartache.

The Cold Reality Setting In

I now had time to update Nancy on the new information. Claire Mitchell and James Peters were presently in custody, having confessed to the crime. Yes, it was confirmed we were now the

Daniel J. Williams

victims of a crime. Suddenly Nancy got up, walked to another room, and started to let out a high-pitch cry of pain and anguish as she fell to her knees. She then ran to get some bed sheets and started to cover the baby gifts that were still in the living room.

"I can't see this stuff now. There was never a baby!" she cried out. She fell to her knees in tears again as the reality fully set in. The pain she was experiencing, was turning into anger.

This was it. The dream of having a child was just that, nothing more than a dream. Where was the loving God she had placed her faith in? I wanted so much to comfort her, but I had no words of comfort. The truth was I wanted to slither away and grieve, but I had no time. I had a case to work. I also knew she needed this time alone to grieve.

Poor Debbie sat there upset and teary-eyed as well. She too had gone through so much this day. She was as much a victim as we were. I feared this would be just the tip of the iceberg. Her husband Mike was on his way to help her make the long drive back home. This day had to be traumatizing and overwhelming for her.

As I was coming to grips with the fact we were victims of a crime, I knew what I had to do. As much as I wanted to stay in the fight, I had to step aside and let another supervisor take charge of this investigation. As much as there was to do, I was afraid anything further involving me would only serve to taint the investigation. I had often preached to my agents the importance of remaining objective, and any objectivity I had was now gone. It was time to abide by what I had preached for so long.

Just then Sam called. We agreed it was time to transfer the case. He promised me he would ensure the U.S. Attorney's Office would take the matter federally. I knew Sam understood the scope of what needed to be done and would ensure it got done.

Sam and I had made a great team together for nearly seventeen years during our careers. He was the best man at my wedding. He was more than a boss; he was a very close friend and confidant. We always had each other's back. Yes, we would even argue and fight

The Miracle of Kayla

like brothers. Sometimes those arguments would erupt into shouting matches, but they were always followed by who was going to pick up the lunch tab. Sam was the agent I wanted by my side going through the front door to execute an arrest. He had an amazing wit and always maintained a cool head on his shoulders. Together we had stumbled into so many dangerous situations in our early careers, but we always managed to walk away unscathed. I knew I could now walk away knowing my buddy was on top of it.

After I hung up the phone, I briefly smiled. I realized just then I never really spearheaded this investigation like I assumed. All I did was send three outstanding investigators to check things out. They then set in motion this amazing investigative machine called the FBI.

Now was the time for me to stand down whether I wanted to or not. The legal proceedings and case were out of my hands. The FBI was on the case, and I knew they could handle it better than anyone. I had seen this great organization do amazing things time after time, to include the numerous investigations that would never see the light of day.

Still, there was somewhere else I needed to be. I had to be with Nancy, who was devastated and crushed with a broken heart. Yet, I was at a loss on how I could console her grief. Where would I start when I didn't even know how to help myself. I knew this was something only God could do, not me. Yet, I also knew Nancy was a strong, courageous and driven soul. Perhaps it would be her helping to lift me up, rather than the other way around. I could only pray as much.

What I could not shake off was my anger that God had allowed this to happen. At the end of the day, I was emotionally drained and numb. At least for this day, my anger towards God would have to wait.

CHAPTER 11

The Long Night

When all the dust settled from the day and Debbie had left still visibly shaken from the ordeal, I found Nancy just sitting outside staring into the distance with a blank look. It appeared for now she had no more tears. Nancy had never been touched personally by crime. It was something that happened on television but never in her life. She lived in a world where people cared for each other. People were supposed to be generally good, not evil. Trust was the foundation of how people dealt with each other. She had a kind and gentle heart for people. Now she was trying to reconcile the worldview she once knew with the evil one she had just discovered. At the same time, she was trying to find peace in her grief.

Unfortunately, grief was something I had become well acquainted with. I saw it all too often in the victims of the crimes we investigated. I often brought the pain home with me. Most of the time, I could try to shake it off at the front door. But occasionally, there were certain crimes that would steal a piece of me and inevitably poison my heart. I would often tell my agents to never let it become personal. Yet, it was something that I myself seemed unable to do at times, no matter how hard I tried to compartmentalize it. The thoughts of the child I could not save, the towers that would fall on my friends, and the sheer depravity I saw so often, would serve to haunt my dreams.

The Miracle of Kayla

But now I was the victim, and I could not shake the empty feeling it left me with.

The day had passed, and neither of us had eaten. I touched her shoulder and suggested we go out to eat. We were not emotionally capable of performing any task such as cooking. Therefore, we went to a local restaurant, but when the food arrived, we just stared at it. We simply couldn't muster any real appetite. We just picked at our food.

"How could all this have happened," she inquired. She was searching for answers I did not have. I'm not sure, but I also think she was searching my eyes for hope. "Is this it? Is our journey finally over?"

I tried to give an answer, but in the end, I shrugged my shoulders. I had no words of comfort or hope. For the first time in my life, I didn't have anything to say.

When we returned home, we really didn't say much to each other because there was truthfully nothing to say. We were both in a daze. I was trying all I could do to remain strong for her, but I knew I was a complete mess.

Later we got dressed for bed and laid down. We both just stared at the ceiling trying to fathom what had just happened. Was there anything we could hold on to? Was it all a lie? Was hope finally gone? Was everything we dreamed of simply a mirage? Did we simply deceive ourselves into believing what we wanted to believe? Eventually, I drifted off to sleep.

About 3 a.m. I woke up and turned over to discover that Nancy was not there. I got up to look for her. I came to what would have been the baby's room, and there I saw Nancy sitting in a chair with her arms propped up on the crib railing. She was just staring into an empty crib listening to baby lullabies over and over again as the mobile moved around at the top of the crib. She sat there in tears realizing this crib would never be filled. A void would remain in her heart for a child who would never come. I harbored those same feelings. Mitchell and Peters did more than steal our money; they

Daniel J. Williams

stole our hearts, dreams and trust. They stole our child…at least that is what it felt like to us!

But how could I possibly begin to console this woman I loved so much? In a way, this was my fault. I had harbored an innate suspicion things were not as they appeared from the start. I had a gut instinct sharpened by years of service to the FBI. I even saw an report a few days earlier that should have confirmed my intuition. Yet for the first time in my career, I had failed to act, and that failure to act was now responsible for the broken heart of the woman I loved.

As the mobile kept turning and the lullabies kept playing, I could only look at the woman who couldn't take her eyes off the empty crib. I was the one who continued to pursue this hope. I put her in this position. Subsequently, I was the one who was responsible for the crime I brought to our doorstep. I was an FBI agent who had taken an oath to serve and protect. I was the one who came to the aide of victims. I was never supposed to be a victim. I couldn't even protect the one I love.

At that moment, my heart was breaking. I wanted to put my arms around her and comfort her. Instead, I stood frozen at the door, desiring her forgiveness for not protecting her heart, but too afraid to ask for it.

I slowly walked away without her knowing I was there. I wanted to leave her to her grief, hoping the time would come when I would find my own time to grieve. But when I returned to bed, I found myself looking at the ceiling, asking myself wasn't God supposed to give us no burden greater than we could bear. Now I knew that old saying was just a myth. Seeing Nancy gazing into the empty crib was just too much for me to suffer. I had not only reached my breaking point, I had crossed it. I slid out of my bed onto my knees. I was hurting so much I didn't even know what to ask. I just knew of God's promise, "Come to me, all you who are weary and burdened, and I will give you rest." (Matt 11:28) Yet, I had no elegant prayer to offer up because

The Miracle of Kayla

I was completely broken, lost and confused. The only words I could spit out were, "Help me, God!" Surely God would not have time to listen to such a pathetic prayer, never mind answer it, I conjectured. But it was all I had.

My FBI Family

The next day, Nancy and I took off from work. No one had expected us at work since we were supposed to be home with our new baby. Plus, we knew we were not capable of dealing with reliving the events from the previous day.

The phone rang. It was my Support Service Technician (SST) Melissa Shawver who was my right hand. While I may have supervised the squad, it was Melissa who kept it running. More importantly, she had a knack for keeping me out of trouble. She was always the calm voice I would hear before I got ready to verbally take someone's head off, especially at headquarters. She was a young, bright, self-starter who kept all my agents in-line to make sure they didn't miss a deadline, or drop some edict I had put out. To say Melissa was extremely organized was an understatement. I was truly blessed to have someone like her working for me. I often thought she should be an agent. There were times when I thought she should be sitting in my chair because she was so good at everything she did. Everyone on the squad knew when Melissa spoke, she was speaking on my behalf. I made sure everyone knew it.

She called to find out how Nancy and I were doing. I told her about the night before and how difficult it was. I commented I needed to get rid of the all the baby stuff. It all served as a painful reminder, but I had no idea where to even begin. The task just seemed so overwhelming at the time.

That comment was all it took. Suddenly, Melissa was marshaling an army of agents. The next day, they all arrived in their personal

Daniel J. Williams

vehicles and trucks on their own time. They were here to return everything and get our money back.

I asked her, "How do you ever plan to do all this?"

She looked at me incredulously and said, "Shut up and simply sit down and make yourselves comfortable. Don't worry, we have it covered."

Suddenly, Melissa was barking out orders to all these agents, and they willingly complied.

Nancy just sat there amazed. Although she was astonished how Melissa took such control, I on the other hand was not. This was who Melissa was. I learned a long time ago just to get out of her way. I knew whatever task she was undertaking, it was going to be perfect.

Nancy was also stunned that so many people showed up to help. Before we knew it, the crib and everything was disassembled, packed, and ready to go. By that afternoon, there wasn't any trace of evidence a baby was ever supposed to live in the house.

Nancy gave Melissa all the receipts she had for each purchase showing from what stores they'd been bought. I briefly thought this challenge might be too much even for Melissa, but the thought quickly passed when I remembered this was Melissa and not someone else.

A few hours later, Melissa and the crew came back. Together, as challenging and overwhelming as this task seemed, they had returned every single item and gotten our money back. All I could do was hug her. She was simply amazing. I could not have done this by myself. She was more than just an employee; she was my dear friend who always had my back.

Until I take my last breath, I will never forget what Melissa and every one of those agents did for us that day. This was our FBI family. They saw one of their own hurting, and they gathered to lift us up.

Melissa Shawver.

CHAPTER 12

A Parade of Possible Victims

When I returned to work, the squad handling the case sent agents down to interview me as a victim witness. I had conducted many victim witness interviews during my career, but I had never been on the other end of the table.

The lead agent was John McLemore, a tall, senior agent who had worked white collar crime for years. He had earned an excellent reputation, and I knew the case would be in good hands when I saw him walk through the door. He and the rookie agent with him were very kind and professional, especially since I was still a wreck. I gave them everything I knew they would need such as the ultrasound, blood work, copies of the checks I sent to Heritage to pay for alleged living expenses, and any other documents that could be used as evidence.

Later that day, I had to sign a bunch of documents from our victim witness specialist, Kim Weems. She had a big heart and was an important part of our team. She was often there with us at a crime scene whether it was 2 a.m., a weekend, or holiday. Kim was very devoted to helping the victims of crimes. She was often the calm

94

The Miracle of Kayla

voice in the storm. I noticed my name and Nancy's were included on one report. Wow, I thought, how unusual was it for the supervisor to sign a victim witness report where he himself was the victim.

When Kim came to see me, she informed me of all the assistance she and the federal government could bring to the table to help us. I had to smile. I'm sure this must have been an awkward moment for her to advise her supervisor of all the things I was already well familiar with. But Kim knew me too well. She realized I would be the last person to take advantage of any of it. She was right, of course. Nevertheless, she was going to make sure I knew she was there for me. I greatly appreciated her desire to help me and how difficult this moment must have been for her.

Every so often, I could see people coming into the office to be interviewed by John and the agents on the other squad concerning the adoption fraud. I wondered if any of them knew why they were here, or if they were about to learn they were the victims of a crime. How were they handling their crushed dreams? It seemed to be a parade of people coming forth. I just wanted to reach out and let them know I understood. Yet, I really had no way of knowing why there were at the office. I could only conjecture. I didn't ask any of the agents, and they never told.

It was killing me not to be in charge of this case and to be intentionally kept out of the loop. Yet, I was the one who said from the start I needed to step aside. How could I complain now? This was a mail/wire fraud case, and I knew it. The white collar crime squad was the right place to address this case. This was precisely the reason I needed to step away. I was too invested. Objectivity had to rule the day. Yet, this opposition of what my heart desired and my mind knew was right would plague me throughout the investigation. I was simply going to have to practice what I preached throughout my long career.

FBI agents are fairly good at compartmentalizing their work life from everything else in their lives. By this time in my life, I had seen and experienced it all. I had been part of the 1993 and 2001

Daniel J. Williams

terrorist investigations on the World Trade Center in New York, the 1996 TWA Flight 800 probe, and numerous other high profile cases. I had worked and supervised some of the most heinous violent crimes and murder investigations. I had seen the tragic outcome of so many child kidnappings that would leave me with a silent rage for the perpetrator and deep sadness for the family. But I had mastered the art of compartmentalization by this point in my career. It was the only way I could find peace with the violent world I lived in.

But for the first time in my life, I could not compartmentalize the loss Nancy and I suffered from the crime committed against us. I was struggling to separate the FBI agent from the victim. How I hated to think of myself as a victim. While I could always empathize with the victims of the crimes we investigated, I was always able to separate them from the crime. How wrong I was!

I invariably assumed if I could bring them justice by arresting their perpetrator, I could bring them closure. In many cases, my heart actually broke for those victims who would never recover from the loss of their loved one. I knew even after I helped uncover the evidence that led to their family member's killer being sentenced to death, they would still struggle to find closure and peace.

Yet, the arrest of the subjects who committed this crime against us brought me little solace. All I could see was the emptiness in my wife's eyes longing for a child who would never come. Despite how much I wanted to heal her heart, I could not.

There is technically no such crime as adoption fraud in federal law. All the federal government had to hang its hat on was mail and wire fraud charges and possibly identity theft. The agents were doing everything they could within the limitations of federal law. I knew it, and I deeply appreciated it.

Months later, Mitchell and Peters plead guilty in federal court. The evidence against them was overwhelming. The investigations conducted by the FBI and other state agencies identified other subjects engaged in similar adoption frauds. Those individuals were later charged separately either in federal or state court.

The Miracle of Kayla

Yet, what all these individuals and separate conspiracies had in common was the fact they preyed on couples like us who desperately sought to have a child through adoption. They also preyed on the agencies that try to offer life as an alternative. They were able to hide behind the cloak of confidentiality and anonymity that the law unintentionally provided them. The family courts that authorized their financial support did not possess the resources to verify their story. Subsequently, a subject could receive several different financial support agreements using different aliases. They were able to further their conspiracy through mail fraud, wire fraud, identity theft, numerous aliases, falsified medical reports, manufactured ultrasounds, and pregnancy pillows that made themselves appear pregnant.

The law also gave the expectant mother the right to change her mind after she delivered her child. It was this protection they used to exploit their crime. It was this loophole that allowed them to walk away untouched. However, the unsuspecting couples were left to wonder why the birth mother was never heard from again after the potential adoptive couples had invested so much financially and emotionally. By suddenly ceasing communication with the agencies, the adoptive couples were left to assume the birth mother changed her mind and decided to keep the baby. What they didn't know was there never was a baby. These predators had exploited this protection of privacy to commit the unreportable crime. The adoptive couples were left seeking closure that would never come.

Many of the victims of their crimes took their life savings, borrowed from their 401K's, or took out second mortgages to finance their potential adoption. But it is the wake of broken hearts that is the true cost of the crimes committed by Mitchell, Peters and other people who engage in such conspiracies. There are now couples who will never again be able to seek adoption because of the financial loss or emotional pain they suffered.

Mitchell and Peters were scheduled to be sentenced in federal court in November 2011. I wrote an impact statement to the judge

Daniel J. Williams

for consideration at the upcoming sentencing. I was all too familiar with federal sentencing guidelines and what the maximum sentence for each would be. I knew my presence in court was not going to change the outcome. Besides, I really didn't want to waste another second on them. I also understood how important it was to write a clear impact statement so the judge could see the crime through the victim's eyes. I also owed it to any other victim out there.

Nancy, on the other hand, wanted to be there when they got sentenced. She wanted to look them in the eye and let them know exactly the pain they caused us and others. Somehow, she thought it would bring her some minor closure to the long ordeal. I didn't have the heart to tell her that her comments would most likely have no impact on them. They were criminals who cared only about themselves. The only thing I believed they were sorry about was getting caught. I had seen it too often in my career. How I wished I was wrong.

On the day of Mitchell's and Peters' sentencing, Nancy and Debbie attended. The judge permitted victims to give an oral impact statement. Nancy was the only one who spoke. The only time Mitchell showed any emotion was during Nancy's address to the court describing the impact their crime had on her. Nancy then looked Mitchell directly in the eyes and asked how a mother could have committed such a heinous crime against another woman whose only desire was to be a mother herself. When Nancy completed her statement, the judge was so moved she gave Mitchell and Peters the maximum sentence of 27 months in federal prison.

It took a great deal of courage for Nancy to speak to the court. She felt compelled to speak for other possible victims who might not have a voice. How I admired her courage. I should have been in that courtroom with her, if for no other reason than to support her. Yet, I let my smug opinion about the power of an impact statement keep me from her side. I was proud of her for taking an important stand and disappointed in me.

98

The Key of Forgiveness

I was finally confronting my own reality. We were never going to have a child! We had arrived at a point that I perceived as the wall of impossibility. We had tried everything and failed. We discovered we could not have children on our own or with the help of science. We discovered we could not adopt because I was simply too old. We believed God had led us down each path so we could have the child he placed on our hearts. Yet, at the end of every step, we found heartbreak and despair.

Could it be God never planted this desire in our heart? Was it really just our desire? Had we lived the last seven years wanting to believe it was his as well? Had we just sacrificed all this time, energy, and money to jump on a roller coaster of hope and sorrow?

I was now knocked flat on the canvas, and for the first time in my life, I didn't seem to possess the will to get back up. This strong-willed, overconfident guy knew for the first time in his life that there was something he could not conquer. I knew I had to summon the courage to get up. Yet, it seemed like the only thing I could do was crawl over to the ropes of the ring, but I didn't have the wherewithal to pull myself up.

Surprisingly, I didn't take much solace from their incarceration. One day I could feel God tugging at my heart. He was now telling me to start praying for Mitchell, Peters, and their families. He specifically placed it on my heart to pray for their salvation while they were incarcerated. My initial thought was God must be joking. I actually started to get mad at him for even asking me to forgive the unforgivable. How could he ask such a thing? Then as I was reading the Bible that very day, I read Matthew 5:44-45: "But I tell you, love your enemies and pray for those who persecute you, that you may be children of your Father in heaven. He causes his sun to rise on the evil and the good, and sends rain on the righteous and unrighteous."

This hit me right between the eyes. Somehow, God seemed to write this verse just for me. God had already forgiven the unforgivable.

Daniel J. Williams

He had forgiven me. He even gave his only begotten Son to pay the debt I could never pay. How could I not be expected to forgive others who had sinned against me. I had to find a way to conquer this wall of animosity I held against them. I knew I could not do it alone, and so I just started to pray as God had commanded me to.

I confess initially I merely went through the motions of praying for them. My prayers were less than half-hearted. At best, they were malicious compliance on my part to God's command. I knew I could not hide from him. He knew my heart better than me. I had no hope of fooling the Creator of the universe, the God who wove the very fabric of my soul.

Yet, I still was waiting for my time to put on the gloves with God. My anger with him was still brewing. He knew that day was coming. I have no doubt he was ready for it. It was never going to be a primetime pay-for-view event. In my foolish heart, I was going to come out swinging because I felt he needed to know what he had put us through, as if he already didn't know.

I was angry at God. He knew this, but it was okay with him because he already knew the outcome. What an outcome it would be! Yet for now, I would continue with my half-hearted prayers.

Slowly over time, the person who my prayers started to change was me. I actually started to feel a compassion for the perpetrators on my heart. Despite their crime, God made it clear when I read Romans 3:23-24: "for all have sinned and fall short of the glory of God, and all are justified freely by his grace through the redemption that came by Christ Jesus." I was no different. My sins were crimes against God himself.

Although they were in jail, my heart was incarcerated by my own animosity towards them. In time, my prayers for them released me from my own prison cell. God had given me the key of forgiveness. Perhaps this was the other reason God wanted me to pray.

I don't know if they ever found salvation. Perhaps I am naive or I have become an unabashed optimist, but I often think what a beautiful ending it would be to this story if they somehow found and

The Miracle of Kayla

took Jesus Christ as their Lord and Savior. If he placed it on my heart to pray for them, then it is not that far-reaching for me to conceive he would have his Holy Spirit lead them to the cross, convict their hearts, and direct them to repentance so they could discover his love, mercy, and grace.

It was for this reason I made the decision to change their real names in this book. If they ever claimed Jesus as their Lord and Savior, I wanted them to know they had been truly forgiven as far as the East is from the West. I would not want this book to haunt or follow them for the rest of their lives. I would want them to have a new start without having to constantly look over their shoulders at a reminder of their past mistakes. I wanted them to know I had forgiven them too.

For several years, Nancy still struggled with the pain inflicted by Peters and Mitchell. Often their actions caused her difficulty sleeping at nights. This was the first time in her life she had been so close to such cruelty. At times, she expressed disbelief and even anger that I could forgive them so soon. It was haunting her that she could not forgive them as easily. She was disappointed in herself that she found it such a struggle to walk in her faith. Yet, time has a way of healing wounds, and after nearly five years, she found the ability to forgive them. Finally, their crime no longer occupied a place in her heart.

CHAPTER 13

Boxing with God

After the arrest in May 2011, I tried everything I could to find some normalcy in our lives. Shortly afterwards, I suggested we go see an animated movie that just came out. It was supposed to be funny. Although it was a children's movie, neither of us were up for anything crime related or violent. We just wanted to laugh again. It was something we had not done in a long time. While I don't remember the name of the movie, I do remember it made Nancy laugh a few times, along with 600 other kids.

Later, we decided to book a weekend retreat to a very nice resort to take our minds off our despair. When we got there, we would walk around, but conversation was sparse. The vacation did little to help us in the way of mending.

The next several weeks were slow. It seemed like we were in a fog. We were just existing and going through the motions. We would get up, shower, eat, go to work, come home and go to bed. Half the time the phone went unanswered unless it was the FBI. Neither of us really had a desire to converse. Yet, it was not talking to each other that was driving me nuts. At times, I felt I had to walk on egg shells. I was just praying time really would heal all wounds.

I could not let go of our grief, and yet, for some reason, I didn't want to let go of it. It was easier to hold onto it like a precious

The Miracle of Kayla

jewel than to let it go. Somehow holding on to it justified my anger towards God.

One day, while in my car going to work, I started into my usual morning prayer time. Suddenly, a wave of anger hit me. I was angry at God, but I had not yet prepared myself for the big showdown I kept running through my mind. All I knew was I was so angry with him. All the pent up emotions broke through the dam, and suddenly I blurted out, "You are responsible for all this. You planted this desire in our hearts. I tried to be obedient. I tried to live up to your will. All we got was seven years of hope that was snatched away by despair. We gave our lives and fortune trying to make your desire come to life. What did we get for all of it? Sorrow, pain and broken hearts that will never be healed. You left us God! You abandoned us in our greatest time of need! Where are you now? Why do you choose to remain silent?"

What was I doing? Did I not realize again who I was talking to? Did I not care God could strike me down? But I wasn't done.

"God, you can try to remain silent, but I know you can hear me. You are my God! You can do anything! I believe in you. I will never lose faith in you, even if you have lost faith in me and abandoned me. I know you are always true to your word. In Psalms 34:18 you said: 'The Lord is close to the brokenhearted and saves those who are crushed in spirit.' Well, Nancy and I are brokenhearted, but I don't feel your comfort. You said in John 15:7: 'If you remain in me and my words remain in you, ask whatever you wish, and it will be done for you.' Well, Father, I am asking. You might strike me down in the next minute, but I am putting you on notice I will never stop bothering you. Every day, until I take my last breath, (which was probably going to be soon) I will call upon you to deliver us a child. You are my God. I know I am but a worthless sinner. But this worthless sinner will never give up on you. So be prepared Father, for you are going to hear from me every single day."

Okay, I had gotten my anger off my shoulders. What was I thinking? Did I really think my defiant attitude and promise of

103

Daniel J. Williams

pestering him daily was going to frighten him into relenting? Did I somehow try to equate this with Heavyweight Champ Joe Louis telling Billy Conn he could run, but he could not hide? Was I trying to blackmail God with his own word? Here I was, this wretch of a man, boxing with God. What had I just done?

Yet, it was almost as if the Holy Spirit was helping me to place in words the anger I was feeling. It seemed he was helping me to articulate what I could not explain or was too afraid to deal with. Perhaps the real message I needed to know was that it was okay to let go of my anger.

But his silence was deafening. I was left with the feeling he abandoned us. The door was finally closing. I needed to resolve myself to the fact we were never going to have a child. After seven years, I was exhausted and emptied. The dream I felt so certain God had placed on my heart so many years earlier on an airplane arriving in Oklahoma City, was just a mirage.

What I did not understand was God had a plan, and perhaps the revelation of his will for my life wasn't as far off as I imagined. I had been looking at the past seven years from the perspective of the here and now. He saw and planned it from eternity past, present and future.

CHAPTER 14

God Can Make a Way

In late June, 2011, I was back at work going at a frantic pace. I was juggling a myriad of new cases hitting my desk and new directives being sent down from FBIHQ. I knew these new edicts were another overreaction to oversight hearings on Capitol Hill. Yet, these new requirements were going to eat up more of our time and take away the focus we needed to get our jobs done. After reading them, I instinctively knew what to expect as I braced my ears for what was coming next.

Almost on cue, Clay and Todd strolled into my office and strategically perched themselves on opposite sides of my office. How many times during my tenure as their boss had I seen this strategic approach play out, much like two lions ready to move in for the kill. This was a clear sign, based upon past experience, that I was about to endure an inquisition where I would be "tarred and feathered" for something I didn't develop.

However, just like in the past, that little fact had nothing to do with the tribunal I was about to face. It did not matter that I even shared their opinion. I was guilty by association because I was management. In their minds, I had to be a co-conspirator. I represented the "dark side" of the force. Therefore, the truth was not going to get in the way of good "tar and feathering." Despite the fact

105

Daniel J. Williams

we were close friends who would go to lunch almost daily, a trial was demanded. They were here to preside as impartial arbitrators of the evidence, despite the fact they had already convicted me prior to walking into my office. Nevertheless, if it wasn't this, it would be something else they would want to complain about, regardless of whether or not I could change it. This had become part of our daily ritual. It wasn't as if I could put them in my doghouse since they were already permanent residents.

Yet, I believe my two friends understood I was feeling down. Instinctively they knew a good "tar and feathering" was precisely what the doctor would order to pick me up. Therefore, the inquisition went something like this:

"Do you know," Todd started, "how much of our time these new rules are going to eat up?"

Followed by Clay chirping in with, "Who came up with this stupid, crazy stuff?"

"Now there you two go again trying to think," I rebutted. "Once again, you are letting logic cloud your thought process. How many times have I told you two knuckleheads logic has never been part of the mindset in Washington."

"But Dan," Clay said incredulously with a big grin on his face as if to suggest he had me, "you were up there previously for three years making all these decisions that we still have to live with, correct?" (As if to suggest I wrote both the entire FBI and Department of Justice operational guidelines in a mere three years with the sole purpose of making his life miserable.) "You even have your picture prominently displayed right here with you shaking hands with our fearless leader. He even gave you an award for your treachery."

"You know what they say Clay," Todd jumped in. "If the evidence fits ..."

Clay completed the sentence with, "We must convict!"

Why I kept that picture of me receiving the Director's Award from FBI Director Robert Mueller in my office still baffled me. Maybe I was unconsciously keeping it there to initiate the morning

106

banter, or maybe I was just a glutton for punishment. The two of them were sure to bring it up every time they walked into my office. It was as good as throwing red meat to two hungry lions. They were sure to remind me they didn't have any similar picture, as if to prove their innocence.

"Good try, my friend," I retorted in my incisive manner. "I managed to escape my mandatory lobotomy because I was operational and traveling all over the world. The powers that be, realizing they were unsuccessful, sent me here just to make you two miserable. Unfortunately, it has turned out to be the reverse. Now, don't you two have a job to do? Why are you two on my squad again?"

"For the sole purpose of making you look good, Boss," Todd responded like a drone. It was my squad motto that I drummed into their heads daily.

"And who said that West Point education wasn't going to amount to much. You have learned well my friend, but now the lesson must end," I replied.

This was a reflection of our daily banter. It would continue through lunch, surveillance, over the radio, meetings, the wire room, and before we called it a day each evening. It has never ended. Yet, I wouldn't have it any other way. The two of them were top notch agents who would walk through fire for a friend. I had the fortune to count myself as one of them.

They knew I was barely keeping it together. I was struggling to find my purpose with each sunrise. There were so many days strung together where I just didn't want to get out of bed, let alone deal with all the decisions that awaited me in the office. I couldn't shake this malaise I was feeling. This morning ritual was actually a welcomed kick in the rear. They were more than subordinates. Todd and Clay were close friends who had my back, and they were not about to let me wallow in self-pity. They knew how to drag the "fight" in me back out.

Later that day, the phone rang. I initially thought it was either Clay or Todd calling me because they had found a new grievance.

Daniel J. Williams

Instead, it was Debbie Nomura. She wanted to meet with Nancy and me right away. She really would not give me many details, but I told her I would call Nancy and get back to her. If this was another adoption, we were hesitant about latching on to hope again, only to have it snatched away.

Later that evening, Debbie arrived at our home. She had an extremely unusual case to present to us. She said a young, married couple had come to them in the middle of May about placing their unborn child up for adoption. Their names were Hilary and Jonathan. At that time, they had learned she was approximately seven months pregnant, and she was carrying a baby girl due in the middle of July. They had been married close to a year and would soon celebrate their first anniversary. Jonathan was part Native American.

They were two amazingly mature adults who wanted to do the best for their unborn child. They knew at this time in their lives, they were not ready to raise a child. However, through their faith in God, they wanted to give this child to a couple who were seeking to adopt. They wanted a couple who would provide the baby girl with unconditional love and raise her in a Christian home. Both wanted their unborn daughter to have all the love and opportunities possible.

Debbie further explained they had been shown many life books from other couples. The two of them had taken a great deal of time reading each one of the books, some of them several times. This was a major decision for them that they were not going to take lightly. They were praying about it every night. Finally, after much thought and prayer, they had narrowed their choice down to two couples. Debbie exclaimed we were one of those two couples. They wanted to interview both couples before they made a final decision.

Nancy and I just looked at each other. Could this be true? Was there still a chance? Would God do the impossible for us? Debbie asked if we were interested and if we were willing to meet them. The answer was an unequivocal "yes".

Debbie advised us that since the July 4th holiday was fast approaching, she would arrange the meeting shortly thereafter. I

108

The Miracle of Kayla

told her this wouldn't be a problem. We had previously arranged to meet my sister Mary and her son Nathan in Hot Springs, Arkansas. We were looking forward to relaxing and spending a fun time with family. We were also looking for time to just get away and thought this trip would do us good. However, we were willing to make any change necessary to accommodate Hilary and Jonathan. Debbie set the date for July 5, 2011.

Debbie further advised us since Jonathan was a tribal enrollee, this would be a slightly different adoption and often scared off potential adoptive parents. The law required strict adherence to the Indian Child Welfare Act (ICWA) since he was part Native American. She told us that not only did Hilary and Jonathan have to consent to the adoption, but the tribe did as well. There were other requirements to ensure compliance with the IGWA laws; however, her agency would confirm adherence to every element of the law. She told us it was not uncommon for a tribe to file a Motion to Intervene shortly after the birth parents terminated their parental rights. This motion was often filed to protect their tribal rights and ensure the integrity of the adoption process.

She also informed us the couple had already presented with other potential adoptive parents who were Native American, which was required by the ICWA laws. They turned down these couples and were now able to consider non-Native American couples, thus allowing us to be considered.

As the FBI Supervisor who also had responsibility for crimes on Native American land for the state of Oklahoma, I fully understood the importance of protecting Native American rights and traditions. I also understood their right, need, and desire to protect their heritage.

When Debbie left, Nancy and I sat in disbelief. I was not sure if we would ever have a child. It was the first time in seven years that it was beginning to settle in my mind this was just my dream and not God's will. Was it possible that God was opening a new door? Could it be God had a plan and now it was about to unfold? Was it about to be revealed in such a way that no one could possibly mistake

Daniel J. Williams

it for anything but the divine hand of God? At the same time, my mind was racing around the idea that this young couple came to the adoption agency in May, which was the month we became victims of the adoption fraud. Was it just a coincidence or God's extraordinary plan from the very beginning of our journey? All the same thoughts were also racing through Nancy's mind. Tears were welling up in her eyes.

Together we took each other's hand and prayed, "God, thank you for renewing our hope and opening a new door. We want to pray for Hilary and Jonathan. We cannot imagine the gravity of their decision. What unbelievable love they must have for their unborn child. Your child, Father. No matter what their decision is, even if they choose the other couple, we want to lift them up to you, as well as this baby girl. You are the God of all things. You are the God of the impossible. The impossible is what you and only you can do. We have come to an impossible wall we cannot breach. There is nothing we, anyone else, or science can do. Therefore, we come humbled before you. Yet Lord, let it be your will and not ours. Your grace is sufficient for us."

CHAPTER 15

The Interview of a Lifetime

Mary and Nathan Mitchell.

It was the July 4 th weekend. We were now visiting with my sister Mary and her son Nathan in Hot Springs, Arkansas. It had been an unbearably hot summer, so it was nice to relax in an area where the heat wasn't as stifling.

It was good to catch up with my sister. The two of us had always been close, and there had never been any secrets between us. She had continually been supportive of us over the last seven years, especially during the adoption fraud. She too was adopted, and this

Daniel J. Williams

helped inspire us to pursue adoption. I was always grateful God had blessed me with such a wonderful sister. Even to this day, I can picture my father throwing her up in the air at three-years-old and catching her and then pressing their cheeks together as they laughed whole-heartedly.

How I wished she could remember him, but she was too young. Perhaps one day, I thought, she would find solace in knowing she would get to touch his face again and feel the love he held for her in his heart. How often I wished she could see herself through my father's eyes. I often wondered how would she react when she was re-introduced to her earthly father by her heavenly Father.

How Dad would have loved her son had he still been alive. I could sketch out in my mind how he would take Nathan aside and say something to the effect, "Son, it's time you learn how to play chess. It is a game that will help you understand life. It will teach you how to think outside the box and strategically plan ahead."

During dinner one night, I shared with her the latest events and told her how excited we were by the prospects. I also told her we were afraid we might somehow not measure up. She said that would be impossible, but I knew she was my baby sister. She was always going to support me.

Our meeting with Hilary and Jonathan was set for the afternoon of July 5th. Our plan was to leave Hot Springs early that morning to meet with them later that day. When Nancy and I woke up on July 5th, both of us were clearly preoccupied with packing and getting ready.

When we met Mary and Nathan for breakfast, Nancy and I had a hard time focusing on eating. Our minds kept drifting to the interview scheduled for later that day. Nevertheless, we managed to enjoy the conversation we were all having around the breakfast table.

A short time later, I checked my phone and realized I'd missed a call from Debbie. I quickly tried to call her back, but I was not getting a very good signal. Therefore, I stepped outside the restaurant, but even then, I could barely hear her because of all the cars passing by.

The Miracle of Kayla

"I'm heading to the hospital. Hilary has gone into labor," she replied.

The noise made it hard to hear. Did she say Hilary had been taken to the hospital? "I thought she wasn't due until the middle of the month," I inquired. I was shouting over the phone so Debbie could hear me. "What do we need to do?"

"You are welcome to come to the office, but I am certain we will not have a meeting today. I'll have more information by the time you arrive. However, the meeting will have to be postponed to another time."

I immediately ran back inside the restaurant to inform Nancy, and we rushed back to our room. After Mary helped us pack our car, we checked out. As Mary walked us to the car, she could clearly see we were nervous and anxious. She gave each of us a long hug, then she and Nathan waved goodbye as we set off on what could be the moment that would change our lives forever.

When we finally arrived in the agency office, we got caught up on the news. Hilary was still in labor. This was no false alarm. She could deliver any minute. It was clear there would be no interview today. Hilary would be completely exhausted and would need her rest. Debbie told us to head on home, and she would call us.

Later that evening, Debbie notified us that Hilary had given birth to a beautiful baby girl. Hilary and Jonathan asked if we could meet with them at 9 am the following morning. Debbie advised us they would interview the other couple not long after we were finished.

Nancy and I then gave thanks to God for Hilary's safe delivery and the birth of this child. We prayed for the other couple who would follow us. We knew they had to be as anxious as we were. We prayed that God would give Nancy and me wisdom and peace about whatever outcome would transpire the next day.

We then set the alarm clock for 5 am and went to bed. I am not sure either of us got much sleep that night. I spent most of the night looking at the ceiling and wondering what the future held. I

113

Daniel J. Williams

was perplexed with so many emotions racing through my mind. A transformation was taking place inside of me. After all we had been through over the last seven years, I was finally understanding I was not in control. I never was. Tomorrow, just like today and yesterday, belonged to God. I was just learning how to let go and give my fear and concerns to him. Somehow I found comfort in this new epiphany.

On July 6, 2011, the alarm clock went off at 5 am. If I got even an hour of sleep, I would have considered it a full night's rest. But I was used to days without sleep. I had briefed the FBI director and the U.S. House and Senate intelligence staff with no sleep whatsoever. I have interviewed famous people without having slept. And no matter what their position was in life, I was never afraid to talk to people. But this day was not like any of those other times. When the alarm went off, I could sense this day was going to be different. This was the interview of a lifetime. It was certainly the most important one I had ever been on.

I looked over at Nancy. It was easy to see she was a complete mess. She was so nervous she could barely find the things she needed. Her hands were shaking, and I could see the sweat on her brow even though she had not gone through her morning workout. When I looked in the mirror, I found I was not doing much better.

Finally, we were dressed and off to the meeting at the hospital. During the two-hour drive, there was little conversation. We knew how important today was and wondered out-loud how things would go. Although we knew God would be with us, we were still nervous. We just spent the rest of the time in the car listening to the radio.

We arrived early. We parked the car, but as soon as we got to the lobby, Nancy went to the bathroom and threw up. She was so nervous, she was shaking. I put my arms around her and tried to comfort her by making her laugh. I have always been able to make her laugh. Maybe that was one of the things she appreciated in me. She was still nervous, but she settled down.

How I was not shaking, I do not know. I guess my job had taken

The Miracle of Kayla

me into dangerous places so often, I had become anesthetized by it by this stage in my life. Oh, I had butterflies in my stomach, but I had finally learned how to control them by now.

A little while later, Debbie came into the lobby. She said Hilary and Jonathan were doing fine, and the delivery went well. She said the baby was also doing well and had spent the night in the room with them. Debbie informed us we would be meeting them in the hospital room. We would be able to see the baby there as well.

Wow, I did not expect this, but it was great. I held Nancy's hand as we followed Debbie. When we walked into the room, the first thing my eyes saw was the baby. She was absolutely the most beautiful thing I had ever seen in my life. Debbie then introduced everyone. We started off with small talk. We naturally inquired how Hilary and Jonathan were holding up. If we were exhausted, we definitely knew they had to be.

We talked about each other's interests. It turned out we shared many. They were Green Bay Packer fans like Nancy and her parents (Green Bay was my second favorite team behind the New England Patriots), and they loved SciFi. Eventually, they started to ask us a lot of question about ourselves. It was clear they knew our life book forwards and backwards.

As we talked, I could not stop looking at the baby. The green pacifier was almost a quarter of the size of her adorable face. She was so tiny. Every so often, she would let out a little whimper and go back to sleep. I would occasionally glance over at Nancy who was also looking at the baby. I wanted so much to ask if I could hold her, but I was not sure if that was appropriate. I knew Nancy wanted to ask as well. I think they saw our desire to hold her, and they graciously offered us that opportunity. Since I was the closest, I reached down to pick up the baby.

There I was, holding this beautiful, tiny little creature. In an instant, this little bundle stole my heart. She even opened her eyes as I held her close to my body and appeared to smile a little bit. Was it possible you could instantly fall in love with someone you just met? I couldn't take my eyes off of her. I carried on our conversation, but I was lost in this child's eyes. I could feel her little tiny heartbeat. Her hand was smaller than my little finger. She was truly an angel from God, and for that moment in time, I got to hold his newest little angel.

I could tell Nancy was dying to hold her too. While I didn't want to give her up, I placed her in my wife's arms. Nancy too was lost in the moment. She looked so beautiful and at peace holding this little angel. We continued to share the baby back and forth during our conversation.

Then the time came to leave. But before I left, I thanked them on our behalf for considering us as possible parents for their special little gift. I told them I knew they had such a difficult decision to make. Yet, I wanted them to know whatever decision they made, we hoped they would find peace in knowing God was with them, even if their choice was not us. I wanted them to know whatever their final decision was, I held them in such high esteem for the amazing love they had for this child. As we departed the room, I still could not take my eyes off of this little angel.

What I did not tell them was everything we had just been through. I wanted them to make their decision based on what they thought was best for the baby. I did not want to introduce pity into their decision.

Debbie escorted us out of the room. We thanked her for all she had done for us. She had walked alongside of us during this long, at times, painful odyssey. In fact, we would not have had this moment, no matter what the final outcome would be, without Debbie. I have no doubt she had shared in our pain. But now her obligation was with this child and Hilary and Jonathan. It wasn't with us. We knew it. It was the way it should be.

When we got back to the car, we again prayed. Not just for us, but for the couple behind us. We prayed for Hilary and Jonathan. But most of all, we prayed God would grant them the wisdom to do his will for this child. We were content. We found peace in wherever God was going to lead them. We thanked him for his grace and giving us this moment to treasure in our hearts forever.

Hilary and Jonathan Padgett.

CHAPTER 16

The Wait

Over the next two nights, no call came from Debbie. We knew Hilary and Jonathan had a major decision to make. One that certainly could not be made in a few hours. We were beginning to assume they had chosen the other couple. Whatever happened, it was God's will. We could ask for nothing more than his will be done. We prayed not only for ourselves, but also for Hilary, Jonathan, and the other couple.

There was nothing more we could do. It was out of our hands. Therefore, Nancy and I got up to go to work like it was any other day. At least that's what we told ourselves.

When I arrived at the office, we had all kinds of things breaking loose. There was a good tip on a fugitive, the opening of several new cases, meetings scheduled with the heads of various law enforcement agencies, reports awaiting my signature, and calls waiting for me from FBIHQ. Plus, the boss wanted a briefing on where we were on a major gang case. At some point, I had to prepare for a career board I was selected to sit on later that week. It was a typical day in my life. I had reached the pinnacle of my career. I had accomplished just about everything I set out to do. I had been the recipient of some of the highest awards in federal law enforcement. I could do the job forwards and backwards blindfolded.

118

The Miracle of Kayla

So why was I having such a difficult time focusing this day. People would walk in and out of my office to brief me on something, but when they walked out, I would ask myself, "What did we just talk about?"

Later, I sat down to do a file review with one of my agents. A file review is a procedure where the supervisor reviews the case work of an agent and makes suggestions, comments, and provides direction on what the agent still needs to do to make a solid case.

How I hated file reviews. The truth was I did them every day with each agent informally. I knew exactly what they were doing at any given time. I would discuss cases with my agents daily. I was out there with them on the street, whenever possible. I never had to guess what they were doing on any single case they had open because I was often involved in it.

File reviews were a requirement by FBI regulations and part of the FBI inspection process. But I was never a supervisor who "managed by inspection." I thought the reviews were not only a waste of my time but that of my agents as well. I knew I was maliciously compliant in conducting file reviews. I also knew we were considered one of the finest Criminal Enterprise/Violent Crime squads in the FBI, and we had the stats to back it up. Our squad and task force had more accomplishments than most of the bigger squads in bigger field offices.

Today I was just trying to keep my mind off of the decision Hilary and Jonathan were about to make, but I couldn't even focus on this file review. Therefore, I told the agent we would pick up where we left off at another time. I naturally had no intention of ever doing that, but I didn't want the agent to walk out thinking I had wasted his time, which I just did. I have no doubt he left wondering what he did wrong because I rarely conducted a full file review.

The Call

I looked at the clock. Had time suddenly stood still? Any other day, there weren't enough hours in the day, but today the clock barely moved.

Later that afternoon, when I was sitting at my desk, the phone rang. It was Debbie. I let it ring a few times so I could take a deep breath and steady myself for what she was about to tell me.

"Are you sitting down?" she inquired. *Oh no! This was not going to be the news I was silently hoping to receive.* "They picked you and Nancy. You are going to be parents!"

I nearly dropped the phone in disbelief. I was trying to speak, but I had a huge lump in my throat. I could feel my eyes beginning to water up.

Debbie was so excited for us. I could hardly contain my own excitement. Could this really be happening to us after such a long journey? Was the impossible really possible? Did God just do the impossible? Debbie then went over the legal hurdles that we still had to maneuver. She inquired if we had picked out a name. Nancy and I had discussed this often. We wanted a name that honored God. We had picked Kayla as a first name, which meant "pure; beloved by God". We picked Faith as the middle name because it was our faith in God that brought us to this moment.

After Debbie and I ended our conversation, the first thing I had to do was call Nancy. How was I going to tell her this amazing news? How was I going to tell her about the amazing gift Hilary and Jonathan had given us? How was I going to tell her about the unbelievable gift God had just given us?

Nancy had been through so much over the last seven years, physically, emotionally, and spiritually. Her life had been a roller coaster ride, yet she never lost her faith in God. She had carried this dream of having a child since we committed ourselves to it the day I flew home from Washington. Now, after all this time, I possessed the news that was literally going to rock her world.

The Miracle of Kayla

I had to tell her immediately. When I called, she was driving down the road. "Nancy, can you pull the car over? I have something I need to tell you."

I could hear her voice begin to break with anxiety. "Please, please, tell me," she said with a quivering voice as she pulled the car into a parking lot.

I was initially going to play elusive and make her guess, but I knew from the shaking in her voice that was a bad idea. "I hope you are ready, because as of today, you are going to be a mommy!"

She just broke down sobbing. She was going to be a mother. It was just beginning to register with her. It took her several minutes before she could speak. What she couldn't see were the tears flowing from my eyes, but I could hear the joy in her voice. When she regained at least some amount of composure, she hit me with a barrage of questions. I tried to field them as fast as they came. It was clear we had so much to discuss. It was also clear we had so much to do. We needed to build a nursery again, buy clothing and baby formula, stack up on diapers and so much more. We had to tell the world. We agreed we would go over everything later that day.

I was still filled with excitement and disbelief. God was great! The impossible was just an everyday thing for God. Meanwhile, there was another group of people I had to tell—my FBI family sitting outside my office. They had been there to share in our ordeal. I had not told them or anyone else about this new opportunity. I was frightened it could fall through again. I couldn't bear to expose my despair once more if it didn't work out. But now I had to tell them. First, I had to wipe the tears from my eyes.

I tried to regain my composure, then walked out of my office to deliver the wonderful news. When I entered the squad bay, Mitch, Melissa, Kim, Doug Samuels, Doug Frost and Andy Kerstetter were all sitting there by Todd's and Clay's desks discussing a case. I must have been beaming from one ear to the next when I appeared. I'm sure they could see the euphoria in my eyes that unfortunately were getting a little glassy looking. I initially tried to come off as

Daniel J. Williams

if nothing was going on and to jump into whatever conversation they were having. But I couldn't hide my joy, and they were trained investigators. It took them all of two seconds to know I had good news.

Mitch looked at me and said, "Boss, you look like the cat who ate the canary. Tell us what's up!"

They wanted to know immediately. I was going to try to start from the beginning and tell them everything, but before I realized it, I just said, "I'm going to be a dad." And with that I would feel a tear roll from the corner of my eye. Darn! I tried to quickly wipe it away with my shoulder so I could maintain my tough guy persona. "Allergies are really getting to me," I tried to feign.

Suddenly, the whole squad started to clap, and each one came up to shake my hand or hug me. Other agents and support personnel started to gather around as well. They insisted I tell them the whole story. They sat there and listened intently. I could see some of the women were starting to tear up as I told the story and what God had just done in our lives. They were all genuinely happy and excited for me.

After that I contacted my sister, the rest of my family, and the people in our church who I knew were praying daily for us as well. Mary shouted out with excitement as I told her the news over the phone. Next I reached out for my buddy Mike Roach. Mike was all choked up when I told him the story. I then had to run upstairs to tell my good buddy Sam. He of all people knew what we had gone through. He just reached over, shook my hand, and gave me a hug. A short time later, Gary Johnson called me from FBIHQ to congratulate me. It took the news less than an hour to make it to him. His phone call meant a lot to me. I must have retold the story ten times by the end of the day.

Taking Home Our Blessing

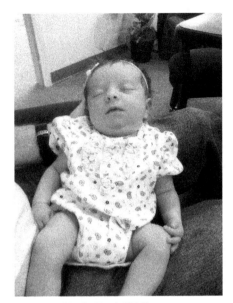

Kayla Faith Williams.

We were so ecstatic when the time came to bring Kayla home with us. When Debbie placed her in Nancy's arms, I felt like God took my breath away, at least for that instant. Nancy cradled our little blessing in her arms as I huddled the two of them in mine. As we started to engage in baby-talk, suddenly the newest member of our family opened her eyes to gaze at the two odd oblong shapes in front of her making strange but soothing sounds. She in turn made a cooing sound in response, and even though I knew a newborn was only capable of a reflex smile, it stole our hearts anyways.

This was the day we had waited to experience for seven years. A simple reflex smile and a little coo would steal our breath away. This moment was the unimaginable reward after our long seven-year journey. Tears were flowing down Nancy's face by now as she coddled our little angel, and yes, tears were welling up in my eyes too.

It was then Mike Nomura put his hands on us as a family and

Daniel J. Williams

prayed over us. No words ever sounded so sweet as when Mike called out for God's blessing on our little family. We had taken so many pictures of that moment in the office at Heritage Family Services, but they all seem like a blur to me now. Yet, forever etched into my mind was the moment I got to place my protective arms around my wife and daughter.

Before we left, I gave Debbie Nomura a big hug and thanked her for walking this journey with us. This moment would not have happened had God not used her to bring Kayla to us.

On the way home, Nancy sat in the back seat while Kayla slept in the car seat. Occasionally, I would glance in the mirror to see her ogling over Kayla. No one deserved this moment more than her. She had endured so much during the last seven years. How I admired her courage and faithfulness during this odyssey. She had never taken her eyes off of God's plan, and now that blessing was asleep in front of her.

I never realized how happy I would be settling for an apartment overlooking a dumpster in the back of a store in Monroe, Louisiana. Little did I know how meeting the beautiful girl next door on the steps leading to my apartment would change my life forever.

When we returned home, Kayla's little eyes opened as we unlocked the door. We knew she was hungry, so we took turns feeding her as our little dog Beebers sat down beside us. Occasionally, he would tip his head to the side trying to figure out what it was we were holding and making such a fuss about.

Eventually, we walked her to each room of the house to show her where she would live. Finally, we took her to the room that would be all hers. We realized it seemed like a frivolous undertaking since she couldn't see more than fifteen inches away. Yet, in our hearts, it was important to take that time to show her the house that was hers. The house she would look back on one day in the distant future and say, "There is the house where God surrounded me with love and developed the person that I am today."

Finally, when night settled in, we changed Kayla again and

124

The Miracle of Kayla

swaddled her before placing her down in her new crib. She briefly looked up in our direction before her eyes closed to fall asleep. What a big day this must have been for her.

After making sure once again the baby monitor was fully working, I came back to find Nancy gazing upon her beloved baby from the bedroom door. I snuck up behind her and wrapped my arms around her. "I am not sure there could be a more blessed man in the whole world than I am right now," I muttered.

She snuggled her head in my arms and together we spent the next thirty minutes looking at our sleeping child as we tried to fathom how quickly this day had passed. God, in his time, had answered our long awaited prayers.

CHAPTER 17

The Easiest Decision I Ever Made

Nancy and Kayla.

It didn't take long for me to be where I wanted. There we were holding our daughter, Kayla Faith. She was so beautiful! We were

The Miracle of Kayla

so blessed! Nancy, Kayla and I were now a family. Family! Until this moment, I never realized how beautiful and wonderful that word was. It suggested so much — love, caring, support, joy, togetherness, and so much more. What a delight it was to see Nancy holding Kayla. She was almost glowing. I longed for years to see that smile return to her face.

When I looked into this little girl's eyes, I could suddenly see a future I could not have seen a month ago. I knew exactly at this moment what I wanted and needed to do. I had to retire from the greatest job in the whole world to pursue the only job I really ever wanted to do. I always thought the bureau would have to walk me out the door when I hit the mandatory retirement age. I pictured myself kicking and pulling at the door to get back in. I always told people jokingly the FBI would get my badge and gun when they pulled them from my cold, dead hands. I could never imagine anything else I wanted to do more until this moment.

I could not take my eyes off of Kayla. She was this tiny bundle of love. Gazing into her eyes, all I could see was the future. I did not want to miss one moment of it. I wanted to be there when she experienced all her "firsts" in life — rolling over, sitting up, standing and walking. I wanted to be there when she said her first word "daddy." Okay, maybe I was a little presumptuous on what her first word would be.

Nevertheless, I could imagine playing with her on the floor and teaching her the alphabet, numbers, and shapes. In my mind's eye, I saw us playing chess, practicing the martial arts, watching the Oklahoma City Thunder and attending the Daddy/Daughter Dances. Yet, the things I envisioned the most were all the wonderful stories God would write on her life.

What an honor it was for Nancy and I to be God's surrogate to raise his daughter. There was no greater responsibility he could have charged us with. He had now given us a new job, one he had whispered into my ear so many years ago on a plane arriving in Oklahoma City from Washington, D.C.

Daniel J. Williams

My new job seemed so overwhelming. Was I prepared and ready for such a challenge? I could suddenly feel God whispering to my heart. "It may seem overwhelming, but I am there to help you. When you are unable to be there, I will be. I am always there. You see, she is my daughter, and as much as you love her, I love her even more. You will invest the rest of your lifetime in her. I have invested the rest of eternity." Okay, still not that burning bush fireside chat I keep looking for, but it brought an unbelievable peace to my anxious heart.

There was no doubt or second thought in my heart. I would turn my retirement paperwork in the following week and retire on September 30, 2011. I was now a full-time dad. Wow, another beautiful word that suddenly took on a new meaning. Dad!

I turned my paperwork in the following week. People from all over the FBI called to congratulate me. My squad was very happy for me. They knew how long I had waited for this day. I think they expected it all along. I could tell some were a little sad. I could see a few teary eyes. I am not sure it was because they would miss me or because they had been counting down to this day since I arrived.

I would miss working with them too. While I would not necessarily miss the circus, I sure would miss the clowns. And yes, whether or not I would ever admit it, I would at times miss the circus too.

CHAPTER 18

The Miracle

The legal process was moving along. Jonathan and Hilary just had their final court appearance to terminate their parental rights. Nancy and I could not imagine what they were going through. I have no doubt it was the most difficult decision they have ever made. They were in our prayers daily. How could we ever truly thank them for such a precious gift!

Jim and Terry Toedter holding their granddaughter.

Daniel J. Williams

Nancy's mother, Terry Toedter, flew up from Florida as soon as she received the news. She was a godsend. It was like learning at the foot of the master. She knew exactly how to quiet Kayla when she started to cry. She clearly was a pro at this parenting thing, and she taught us everything we needed to know. Her husband, Jim, followed later from Florida to meet his new granddaughter.

Kayla was settling into our house very quickly. She truly had become the princess of the house. Our little dog Beebers would not leave her side, and he stood guard wherever she was. She clearly was the center of attention. Everything revolved around her.

Sleep became a thing of the past, but this was hardly a sacrifice. Every two or three hours, Nancy and I were taking turns getting up in the middle of the night to feed and change her. Within a week, I had become an expert at feeding, diaper changing, burping, swaddling and singing nursery rhymes. Kayla had stolen our hearts. She had her daddy wrapped around her little finger. Our lives would be forever entwined.

One day, I took her into the office to show her to everyone. Immediately, everyone ran to the break room to get a glimpse of this little miracle. They all wanted to hold her, and no one wanted to give her up, especially Brenda Davis. Brenda used to work on our squad before management saw how good she was and moved her to another squad. We often referred to her as our "squad mom" because she would crack down on any agent who didn't comply quick enough with one of my directives. How often I would smile when I would hear her threaten to slap someone silly if they didn't meet my deadline. She would often stop in my office just to let me know she was thinking and praying for us.

Often, numerous other FBI employees would stop in my office just to let me know they were thinking about me. Many knew the impossible had just happened. They could not be more excited for Nancy and me. I took Kayla through the entire FBI office. She didn't even have a security clearance yet! I took her to my office and propped her up on my desk so she could see where Daddy worked.

130

The Miracle of Kayla

Later, the office threw a huge baby shower; only this time, the baby was invited as well. It seemed the entire division, as well as my friend and partner Tommy Terhune and the rest of our OCPD partners, were there. The office conference room was barely big enough to hold everyone who came. I had never been to a baby shower before. This was all new for me.

The ladies in the office had everything organized. They had made several delicious cakes and served all kinds of food and drinks. They had even created a large diaper cake. We had so much stuff it completely filled my SUV and Nancy's car. It was an amazing day that created memories for a lifetime. Memories we will get to share with Kayla one day.

She was the true star of the show. They could not get enough of her. Ultimately, what I truly enjoyed was sharing this moment with these people who had stood by us during this long journey. Kayla was now being officially welcomed into the FBI family.

A few days later, we brought her with us to surprise our Sunday school class at Southern Hills Baptist Church. They were having a party just to get together and fellowship. When we walked through the door with Kayla, they dropped everything they were doing. Many of them had genuine tears of joy as they ran to her.

They had been praying for us for so long. Now they could see for themselves the power of their prayers. Prayers that would lift us up in times of despair. I cannot count how often throughout this journey they had to listen to me continually say, even when all hope seemed fleeting, "I will never give up on God." And yet, during those tough times, I wasn't sure if I believed it myself. Surely the strength and power of their prayers renewed my spirit. Now they were there to see the miraculous power of God and the answer to their prayers.

We only had temporary custody during this time. We still had to wait on a court hearing that would grant us full custody. As expected, the tribe filed a Motion to Intervene. We had previously been told to anticipate it, so we were not surprised when it happened. Nevertheless, it still left a sinking feeling deep in our stomach. I, of

Daniel J. Williams

all people, know motions are just routine. It was not meant to be a statement on our parenting ability or us personally. Many times, a motion is filed to slow things down. It is used to ensure the process is moving in accordance with the law.

It is the tribes' duty to protect its esteemed heritage, its members, and the child. It was also important to ensure every aspect of the ICWA laws were being followed. We knew this, but we could not help being a little nervous. Debbie and Mike Nomura were a great comfort ensuring we had done everything in compliance with the ICWA laws.

We were finally notified there would be a hearing on the motion on August 22, 2011. Our hearts pounded. I think each of us could feel an overwhelming cloud of fear above us.

I knew fear could be one of Satan's greatest tools. It could redirect our focus from God to the world. Yes, we were anxious, but we knew our hope resided in God. This knowledge was where our minds would retreat to when fear started to creep into our hearts.

A Message of Hope

The night prior to the hearing, I was restless and scared. I had a hard time initially falling asleep, but eventually, I started to drift away. I had a nightmare as I tossed and turned. I dreamed they were going to take Kayla away from us. Fear started to consume me at the thought that someone was going to take away the child I loved more than my own life. The one thing I could not escape in my dream was a theme that kept playing out with every toss and turn. *This was not my story. It never was.*

Suddenly, I rose from my sleep and sat up in the bed. The dream seemed so real for a brief second and horrifying at the same time. I knew this dazed and confused feeling well. How often I had been woken up at 3 a.m. by a phone call from the FBI. It would always take me a minute or more to gather myself so I could fully

The Miracle of Kayla

understand what the FBI communication center was going to tell me. I always needed that minute so I could know the details with a clear mind and direct what needed to be done. This moment was no different. Was I just dreaming this night, or was something deeper going on? If so, what was it? Was it possible I was just subconsciously projecting what I was hoping for — God's direct intervention to my prayers? When I saw there was no one in the room, I realized I was just dreaming. Yet, it seemed so real, clear and well, earthshaking.

What was not a dream was the verse that came out of my mouth with no explanation or forethought, "Do not be anxious about anything, but in every situation, by prayer and petition, with thanksgiving, present your requests to God. And the peace of God, which transcends all understanding, will guard your hearts and minds in Christ Jesus." (Philippians 4:6-7)

I am rarely lucid at 3 a.m., but I am definitely not capable of reciting scripture, especially this verse. I had read it many times, but I never took the opportunity to commit it to memory like so many other verses. Maybe what just happened was nothing more than a dream and my subconscious influencing its outcome. The FBI agent in me would have found that an acceptable answer since there was no empirical evidence to suggest otherwise. Yet the Christian in me wanted to believe it was something deeper. Suddenly, an overwhelming peace came over me, and I was able to go back to sleep.

The next day, we got ready to go to court. Yet I was perfectly calm because I knew God had this day. He was writing a story in my mind, and I was content to believe we were the characters in it. I was actually anxious to see how his story would play out.

When we got to the courthouse with Nancy's parents and Kayla, we were summoned into the judge's courtroom where the representative for the tribe was present. I had been in plenty of court rooms in my career and had come to learn, whether it was a state or federal courthouse, they all had a similar nuance and decorum

133

about them. This was no different; however, this was the first time I was in court based on personal reasons.

Our attorney spoke first. The judge followed by asking us various questions that we answered wholeheartedly. I assured him it was our desire to enroll Kayla on the tribal rolls. We wanted her to know her heritage and the nobility of her tribal roots.

Then came the tribal representative's time to speak. She advised the court that the tribe was satisfied and had no issue with consenting to the adoption of Kayla.

Our attorney motioned to the judge to finalize our adoption. He asked us a long list of extra questions, then finalized our long-awaited adoption. Afterwards, he looked down from the bench and congratulated us. Kayla was finally ours! It was the first time I ever got choked up in court. We just held Kayla and each other tightly, while Nancy cried tears of joy. Our long seven-year journey had come to an end. We were now a family. No matter how hard I might try, I could never express the unfathomable joy we had at that moment. I can only say it was a moment I will remember until I take my last breath.

The Revelation

When we returned home, we fed and changed Kayla. The mail arrived, so I went to get it. In the stack was an envelope from the US Treasury. *Oh good grief* I thought. Anything from the government is usually never good (coming from the guy who worked for the government most of his life). I put it in my office and walked out to continue to enjoy my baby girl. We could not take enough pictures. Nancy was just glowing as she held her daughter in her arms. Finally, Kayla started to drift off, and we put her down to nap.

Later, I decided it was time to go into my office and sort through the mail. When I opened the envelope from the government, there was a very large check inside with a letter explaining this was money

The Miracle of Kayla

that belonged to me after the FBI recently settled on a class action law suit. In addition to the original money owed to me, the rest was interest that had accumulated over so many years. Years that began long before the dream of a child that God had planted in our hearts. Suddenly, I looked back at the amount of the check. I stood there paralyzed trying to hold back the flood of emotions. The check was in the amount of everything we had lost during this unimaginable odyssey!

I then leaned back into my chair. For the first time in seven years, God had pulled the curtain back to reveal to me his divine plan. This seven-year journey unfolded exactly as he intended before the dawn of time. This was not my story, or Nancy's story, or even Kayla's story. It was God's story. It was always his story. God does not see our lives unfold in human years. He sees them against the backdrop of eternity.

The cross he gave us was not some divine seven-year punishment. Instead, it was an honor he bestowed upon us so we would have a testimony of his faithfulness and love to give to others. God's stories always involve the impossible, especially when it calls for obedience and faith. Our journey brought forth an unborn child who now graces heaven. A child I will one day meet, and he will know my name even though I never knew his.

God did not need Dan Williams the FBI agent. He needed Dan Williams the victim. It was only as a victim that he could use me to discover this group of individuals who preyed off the desire of others to be parents. It was then he used me in my position as an FBI agent to initiate the process of seeking justice.

God had a plan that always ended in the gift of Kayla. When he set us out on this journey, he placed a cross on our shoulders. A cross that would become a blessing. He knew we would suffer a financial loss. Therefore, his mighty hand already set in motion years before he planted the desire to have a child, the means to cover this loss. And when we suffered the loss of a child through the adoption fraud,

Daniel J. Williams

and all hope seemed gone, he had already placed in the womb of a young woman a gift we would call Kayla.

He gave us a cross, but he was always there to help us carry it. He surrounded us with strong prayer warriors at Southern Hills Baptist Church and my FBI family in Oklahoma City. He asked only for our faith and obedience. Even then, he knew there would be times of doubt and despair. He foresaw the times when this crazy man would get angry and want to square off with him.

Yet, God's love is bigger than our anger and sin. Yes, he had given me more than I could carry. It wasn't because he wanted to see me struggle and fail. God knew I was this extremely self-reliant man who refused to hold onto anything other than himself to accomplish something. Therefore, he used the last seven years to pry open my grip on me, so I would learn to hold only unto him. I finally understood what the words "sweet surrender" really meant. Maybe this was the other lesson my father was trying to teach me while waiting on a box of clams so many years earlier.

He writes his own stories. I believe that may have been the real take-away from the dream I had the night before we adopted Kayla. We are just the tablets he writes his story on. He will take us to places we could never imagine.

In this moment, as I just sat on my chair looking toward the ceiling, I finally understood when God placed a cross on our shoulders, he was giving us a great honor and blessing. Our blessing, testimony, and miracle was a little angel we called Kayla.

CHAPTER 19

My Last Day

Samuel Macaluso.

Not long afterwards, I would retire from the FBI on September 30, 2011. The night before, I stood alone looking from my office at the now empty squad-bay area. I was usually the first person into the squad in the morning and the last one to leave at night. In my mind's eye, I could see the daily drama that would unfold here. Drama that we called routine. I could remember the day I entered

Daniel J. Williams

Quantico, my first case, the long hours, the times laden with danger, and the countless lives we saved. But mostly, I recalled all the great people I had the honor to work with. I would keep them with me in my heart forever. When I turned off the lights for the last time, I knew I was starting a new chapter in my life.

The next day was my retirement party. I was shocked by all the people who came. The room was filled with dignitaries and numerous agency leaders. My good buddy, Sam, served as the master of ceremony. Gary Johnson, who was on a temporary assignment, had even flown in from Washington, D.C. to attend my farewell. There were numerous speeches, plaques, and gifts given by the other agency leaders that I will cherish for a lifetime. Doug Samuels, my bank robbery coordinator, even went to the point of composing a poem that highlighted my career in twenty plus verses. It had everyone, including myself, on the floor laughing. They had even arranged a video-cast from agents in other divisions wishing me a great retirement. Front and center of the podium was my legendary doghouse. However, I was the only one in it.

My protégé, Clay, presented me with a gift from the squad that I will treasure for a lifetime. But Clay would not be Clay if he didn't take one more poke at me before I left. He had gotten his hands on the video of me crashing the bureau car through the front gate years earlier because I had simply forgotten to swipe my FBI lanyard on the gate key pad. To my horror, he showed the video to everyone in the audience. Somehow, he managed to play it it slow-motion. Naturally, he had arranged it so it would play over and over again.

I would have done the same to him. I can't count how many times in my career where I pulled a similar prank. It is the odd way we in law enforcement bond. Unfortunately, I was the one who crashed the gate and not him. Even more horrifying, he had recovered the tape recording. This meant I would have to relive this moment every time I saw him.

I guess the only solace I could take from this moment was Clay got all choked up at the end. Being able to say I finally made Clay cry

The Miracle of Kayla

was something I had on my bucket list. Getting choked up would be sufficient enough to check it off. Plus, I had it on tape!

Finally, the boss, Jim Finch, who was the former assistant director of the FBI, presented me with my retired FBI credentials. I have served under many outstanding people in my career, but Jim was clearly one of the best. He always presented a calm demeanor, even when I would come into his office to complain about everything under the sun. Yet, he was usually supportive of every crazy idea I came up with because he trusted me. If ever a man personified the FBI motto of fidelity, bravery, and integrity, it was James Finch. However, the moment he presented me with my new retired credentials, I could feel a lump develop in my throat. This was it. All of these years had come down to this moment.

It was now my turn to speak. I didn't really have anything prepared. I always found it easier to shoot from the hip. I thanked them all for honoring me by being there. While I talked briefly about things in my career, I mostly talked about them. I wanted this moment to be about them. They were the future of the FBI, not me. I wanted them to know how much they meant to me. I talked about the FBI and our motto of fidelity, bravery, and integrity. I talked about how those words were the cornerstone of every case we opened and every action we took. When the wolf approached, they were the ones who would run to protect the sheep. When others would flee, they were the ones who would run to the danger. And when the enemy was at the gate, they were the ones who would run to defend it.

What an honor I had to be part of such a great tradition for so long. Now I was stepping aside to stand with the many agents who had gone before me. Men and women who had developed the legacy of the most respected law enforcement agency around the world. And like them, I would now be on the sidelines cheering on those agents and FBI personnel still fighting to keep our nation safe. All of us, present and past, were forever linked to this amazing FBI family.

We are bound forever by fidelity, bravery and integrity until the day we take our last breath.

But as I was finishing my closing remarks, I could see my beautiful wife with tears of pride looking back at me as she held our bundle of joy. While I knew Kayla would never remember being there to share this moment with me, I would at least have the memory of being able to share it with her. She was the new chapter in my life. She was the gift.

Nancy and Kayla

CHAPTER 20

Lessons from a Child

Kayla

It has been over several years since I retired. During this time, I got to see and film Kayla roll over for the first time, sit up, stand, and take her first steps to me. Her first word was "Da Da," with no prompting or coaching from me, of course.

141

Daniel J. Williams

She is so smart for her age. Naturally, I'm biased, but when she reached Pre-K, she could recite the Lord's Prayer, Psalm 23, John 3:16, and the Pledge of Allegiance. She has known her entire alphabet since she was two. Kayla loves to draw, and she listens intently to every book read to her. She is now capable of reading simple words. I would love to take credit, but she was designed this way by her Father in heaven.

She has a heart for people and does not know a stranger. I confess this doesn't always sit well with her daddy, who constantly keeps his eye on her. One time when we were out at the park, we heard a slightly older child crying. While Kayla didn't know her, she walked over and gave her a comforting hug. She then asked the little girl why she was crying. The little girl said she could not find her mother. Kayla told her not to worry because she and her daddy would find her mother, which we did.

Everyone is Kayla's friend. I sometimes become a little mortified when she walks up to complete stranger and says, "You are my very best friend. My name is Kayla. What is your name?" Sometimes the child doesn't know what to make of Kayla's advances and retreats to their parent's side or looks at her strangely. Others will immediately start to play with their new best friend.

It amazes Nancy and me how this little girl knows exactly how to pull on her daddy's heart strings. Often she will run over to where I am sitting, throw her arms around my neck and say, "Daddy, I love you. You are my hero." I immediately melt like butter. Yet, all she wants is her daddy's heart. She has owned it since I first held her.

Nancy often laughs and says, "One day she is going to throw her arms around you and ask you for a new car. I can already see you folding without a protest. She has her daddy firmly wrapped around her fingers, and she already knows it. Just wait, tough guy, when she turns sixteen. You will be putty in her hands."

The Miracle of Kayla

Kayla

"I'm an FBI agent. I know all the tricks in the book. She can never play her daddy. I've beaten the biggest and toughest," I often protest.

"You keep telling yourself that. Maybe you might even start to believe it. Daddy, you have so much to learn about little girls." She will often shrug her shoulders and say, "Face it, you were outmatched the moment you held her in your arms."

It is usually then I can see my own father becoming an easy push-over for my sister. Have I too become such an easy mark?

I often contemplate Kayla's future. I imagine the things we might talk about. How I look forward to those conversations yet to be. I yearn to hear her tell me about her dreams and her place in the world. The place that was uniquely designed just for her by God. Perhaps there will be a place for me to help her realize those dreams.

I often take the time to write letters to Kayla in order to record something she did or something God placed on my heart at that moment. Perhaps one day, these letters might bring back an old memory of another time and place. I know she is too young to read and understand them now. Yet, the time may come when she may find peace and comfort in these old letters as she experiences her own trials and tribulations.

Every day I have the honor to watch her grow. However, I have also come to see how much I myself have changed and grown. The guy who used to jump and slide over cars at a busy intersection in New York City to chase down an armed fugitive is content to read a book to a young girl. My priorities of protecting national security and apprehending criminals have been replaced by teaching a little girl about life and about God. In turn, I have learned so many lessons from her.

Kayla

Walking with God

I now realize God has used Kayla to teach me about life and where my priorities need to be. Every new milestone she achieves seems to be a new one in my life as well.

The Miracle of Kayla

When she first learned to stand, her little hands would hold tightly onto my fingernails as I tried to teach her how to walk. Whenever she would stumble, I was there to keep her from falling.

How often in my own life have I reached out to hold my heavenly Father's hand as I walk through life. When I would stumble, as I so often have, he was there to keep me from falling.

On the day Kayla took her first steps, she never once took her eyes off of me as I beckoned her to leave the safe harbor of the coffee table. When she summoned the courage, she walked into my awaiting arms. We hugged and cheered her every step. I learned that day that God is always calling us. He calls us to step out of the boat in the middle of a storm to walk with him in faith to do the impossible. His arms are opened wide to receive us. He cheers our every step. I am learning only now to keep me eyes fixed on him.

Boasting in God

When Kayla was approximately three years old, she was playing in my home office while I was delving into research material at my desk. Her curiosity led her to ask me questions about the various awards, trophies, and medals displayed in my office. "Daddy, what does this mean?"

I confess I was giving her cursory answers as I kept plowing through the paperwork. "Kayla, it is just a trophy I won when I was a young man boxing."

She would then move to something else, "Daddy, what does this mean?"

I would momentarily look up from my research and say, "Kayla, it is just an award the FBI gave your daddy years ago."

She continued asking what certain awards meant. I felt like I was being interrogated at times. Yet, at the same time, I felt proud she would even notice.

After she went to bed for her nap, I came back into my office. I

145

Daniel J. Williams

started looking at the awards on the wall. Her persistent questions caused me to ponder what did they really mean. They were now collecting dust. They didn't mean anything to anyone else. At one time, I was very proud of each of them. Now they hold no real significance to me. Perhaps, I thought, they were tokens of a life well-lived. But this thought didn't ring true either.

Suddenly, I was convicted of the sin of pride. Then I started to listen to that still small voice in my heart. There was nothing in this room I could really boast about. The simple truth was I accomplished all these things because God gave me the opportunity, he equipped me to do them, and he carried me over the finish line. All of these awards were really reminders to me of what God did in my life and not what I did.

Once again, my little girl would take her daddy to school with her Socratic method of peppering me with questions. I now use them as an icebreaker to people who visit my house. I use them to tell the story of what God did in my life.

God's Desire to Love and Forgive

One day, I was in the kitchen working on a project putting together a toy I bought for her, which I was extremely focused on. Kayla came up to me and started talking about her doll. She was talking, but I was not really listening. I was too fixed on the project in front of me. Suddenly, she reached up and tugged on my shirt. I could see she had tears in her eyes. She looked up to me and said, "Daddy, you are being rude. It isn't nice to not listen to people when they are speaking to you."

I was so touched and convicted at the same time. I stopped what I was doing and reached down to pick her up. I held her real tight and said, "Kayla, you are so right. Daddy was rude. I am so sorry, sweetheart."

She suddenly put her arms around me. She then embraced my

cheeks with her little four-year-old hands and said, "I forgive you, Daddy. I love you."

Yet, I knew at that same moment, God was using her to teach me. How often does he speak to me, but I am too busy to listen? He waits there to tell me how much he loves me and how he has forgiven me. Yet, I am too busy. I cannot see beyond my front nose. I wonder sometimes, does he too feel sad when I am so rude? God has taught me more in the last few years than I learned in all the years prior. However, I now realize I have let the ebb and flow of life rob me of these special moments when God was making his presence known to me.

Speaking with Boldness

I have also had several of those funny, yet embarrassing moments where my cub would blurt out something in public, and my first reaction was to hide. One day we were in a local restaurant near the university, when four-year-old Kayla told me she had to use the bathroom. I always stood within earshot of wherever she was. I could hear her talking to a young college girl in the women's room. The girl walked out of the bathroom and started walking down the aisle. Suddenly, my cub opened the bathroom door, and to my horror, yelled out in a loud voice, "Ma'am, ma'am, you forgot to flush your toilet."

I then saw the horrified young woman pick up her step to find the exit. My little girl, who had not yet learned to filter what she said, broke into a chase. Running down the restaurant aisle as fast as her four-year-old legs would carry her, she cried out to the woman, "Ma'am, my daddy always says we need to flush the toilet and wash our hands. Ma'am you need to wash your hands."

While I am confident my little girl thought she was being a good citizen, I could only imagine the horror the poor woman must have felt as she made her get-away. The restaurant, crowded with young

Daniel J. Williams

college students, broke out into a roar. My initial desire was to crawl into a big hole to hide, but since that was impossible, I immediately chased down my baby girl and scooped her up in my arms. She of course wanted to inform me of the woman's offense, and how she was trying to be a good girl by attempting to help her.

I was initially at a loss. I had just taught her the day before we should help people if we see them do something incorrectly. Now I had to teach her there was a time and a place to do this, and this was not it. This clearly was not a moment I would ever forget. In her little world, a major offense had just been committed, and valiant action was demanded.

Yet maybe out of the unfiltered words, which could only be spoken by a four-year-old, was another lesson for me to discover. Despite what was an embarrassing moment, Kayla spoke with such boldness. Maybe it was time for me to speak with such boldness about the love of God.

Who I am before God

The greatest lesson I ever learned took place in the most unusual place. On my birthday a few months after she was born, I had placed her on the changing table to change her diaper. She was busy cooing away as I reached over to retrieve a new diaper. Suddenly, she stopped cooing and her eyes locked onto mine. For the next several moments, I became lost in those eyes. The more I kept looking into those eyes, I became overwhelmed with this sense of peace and calm. It was as if God's love was looking back at me and reminding me of his faithfulness even when I had lost all hope.

Then, in the next moment, I saw myself in her eyes. This tiny baby was looking at me dependent upon me for her every need. She needed me to feed her, clothe her, bathe her, groom her, and even change her. She was dependent on me for her every need because she was unable to do anything for herself.

The Miracle of Kayla

All at once, I realized this is how I am before God. I am completely and utterly dependent on him. He feeds me, clothes me, and takes care of my every need. He does what I cannot do for myself. His Holy Spirit interceded for me when the time came that I could no longer pray or couldn't find the words in our darkest hour. He even gave his only begotten Son so I could be transformed from the sin that defined my life.

God had not only given me Kayla, but in this moment, he gave me another transforming gift that altered my life – the gift of true humility. Sometimes, we expect God to alter lives with a flash of light on a road to Damascus. Sometimes, he chooses a simple diaper changing station.

God Completing the Lesson My Father Began

Often, Kayla comes running toward me to jump in my arms. I pick her up, and she gives me a big kiss. We hug each other tightly, and our cheeks embrace for minutes at a time.

It's then in my mind's eye that I can see my dad lifting my sister high into the air. After all these years, I can still see his face across the table looking down at a chessboard. I sometimes find myself scanning the field for his approving nod from the crowd. It has been over forty years since he passed away. Yet, his grip still influences my life. How he would have loved this little girl, and she would have stolen his heart all over again. How she has stolen mine.

How I long to embrace my father to tell him how much I still love him and to thank him for the lessons he taught me. Lessons that would lead me to this moment. How I long to tell him I finally understand what he was trying to teach me so many years ago while waiting for a plate of clams.

"Dad, I finally found my balance. It is that place where you walk in faith and obedience to the will of God. The place where everything takes on the meaning and perspective that God designed.

Daniel J. Williams

A place where you can embrace your little girl tightly to your cheek and see a world you never saw before." I would want my dad to know the fire he ignited in me lives on in this precious child I hold each night. God had completed the lesson he tried to initiate.

When God placed it on my heart to write our story, I wanted to reach out to all those many people struggling to have a child. I wanted them to know they were not alone. God understands their pain even when they might think he doesn't.

Yet, it would be negligent if I was to suggest that God's answer to our prayers is always "yes." Sometimes his answer is "no." In our case, his desire was for us to wait and walk a different path. It was not one I would have chosen to travel, but it was the one God made for us. It was only after we traveled this difficult road that we received his perfect blessing. God's answers are always perfect, even when it is not what we initially desired. He sees beyond the "here and now" to the riches and joy of his eternal kingdom.

I also wrote this book for birth parents, who, for whatever reason, are now considering adoption. I cannot imagine the gravity of the decision they are about to make. Only God can truly understand the depth of their love for the child they carry. He gave his only begotten Son for them, me, and all mankind. I know there are many loving couples longing to provide their unborn child with a wonderful home through adoption. There is a special place in the heart of God for the tremendous sacrifice they would be making. We give thanks and praise every day for the act of love Hilary and Jonathan made for us.

I similarly wrote this book for all those people such as Debbie and Mike Nomura, Nightlight Christian Adoptions, and all adoption agencies. They tirelessly care for birth mothers and couples seeking adoption. Most of all, they seek to provide an alternative to choose life over abortion. I know they walk with those they serve every day, and they share in their pain and joy.

150

Nancy, Daniel and Kayla Williams

CHAPTER 21

My Final Thoughts

It has been over a year since I finished the previous chapter. We have just put Kayla to bed after she read us her favorite book and said her nightly prayers. She is now six-years-old. I stand in awe at all she is capable of doing at this tender age that I could not do until I was in the third grade.

Now, at the end of the day, is my time to relax outside. On a clear night like tonight, you can see the vastness of the evening sky and the glory of God's creation. Here I reflect often on the story God wrote on my heart. I wonder about the stories he may still write. I ponder about the many stories he will write on my daughter's life.

I confess I almost didn't write this book. I was content to let it end at the last chapter without getting it published. I contemplated leaving the single manuscript in my desk drawer for my daughter to find and read sometime in the future. This was my selfish desire until I re-read the last chapter. God gave me a testimony to share. It was not meant to be hidden in a drawer. It was also clear to me that the most important part of the story was missing.

Yet, fear has a way of preventing us from moving forward. It is so much easier to stay within the boundaries of our comfort zone. Each time I thought about it, I would hear a little disparaging voice

152

The Miracle of Kayla

in my mind whisper, "This is not a story anyone will want to read or hear. God doesn't want or need a sinner like you to tell his story."

Moreover, I wasn't crazy about becoming the poster child for victims. However, I knew that thought to be the ugly side of pride. I was also afraid of putting my life out there, to include the intimate details and numerous personal failures, for the world to judge. I was not nor would I ever be a paragon of Christian virtue. While I never questioned my salvation, I still struggled to completely let go and let God take charge of my life, even after all he had done. I was ashamed to admit to the world I got mad at God; I found myself doubting him at times; I struggled with my faith; and I couldn't understand why me.

How often in my life, I have listened to that doubting voice. It has deceived me with true statements and reminded me constantly of all my past failures. I have often wondered how many lives I could have changed if I only had the courage to speak.

I have spent this whole time telling you how God answered our prayer to have a child. Yet, there was still another part of this story I did not write about that needed to be told. It was the story of how God had already accomplished the impossible in all our lives.

Every year I teach Vacation Bible School, I ask the children to look up at where the moon would be in the evening sky. I then have each of them give me their very best effort to jump as high as they can to reach up and touch it. Naturally, their best efforts fall extremely short of the goal I set. Nevertheless, I often smile when I see those children who try their very best to jump as high as they can because they believe they can do it.

I use this demonstration to tell them about the most amazing story of all. I tell them that the chasm between us and God is even greater than their attempt to jump to the moon. The chasm was formed as the result of the sin in our own lives. Our attempts to be the very best we can be, so that we can earn our way into heaven, fall short just like their attempt to jump to the moon. It is simply impossible, but God is in the business of the impossible.

Daniel J. Williams

His love for us is so great that he made a way for us to live with him in heaven for all of eternity. He sent his only begotten Son to us to bridge the gap. Jesus came to pay our sin debt. He did that by placing our sins on himself. He then took them with him to a cross where he suffered and died for all mankind. In three days, he rose again to prove to us he was the Lord of Life, and all we had to do was accept the gift he came to offer each of us.

Salvation is not something we place on the scale of good and evil. It is through God's grace alone that we receive the gift of everlasting life in heaven.

Jesus told us, "I am the way and the truth and the life. No one comes to the Father except through me." (John 14:6) The first time I read this passage I was struck by how simple, yet direct, it was. It left no loophole or any other way. It certainly does not make a provision for us to earn our way into heaven. It is a gift we can choose to accept or decline. Is it politically correct by today's standards? No. But I don't apologize or run away from it. I offer it only as a thought we should all weigh very heavily. Our eternity depends on our answer to his call to each of us.

I know people can debate the issue until the cows come home and still never change their position. It is easy for me to get caught up in the biblical and theological thickets. In the end, it is a personal leap of faith. Yet, there is no single decision that has a greater consequence if you get it wrong. The consequences are eternal.

I long to teach Kayla so many things and to help her realize her dreams. Yet, my greatest desire for her is to receive Jesus Christ into her life as her Lord and Savior. It is the most important decision she will ever make. I want her to understand Christianity is not a religion, but a relationship. She doesn't have to engage in the frivolous effort of trying to reach up to God by being perfect. God, who is perfect, loved her so much he reached down to her. He already paid the price for her. Through Jesus, she was redeemed for eternity. She has only to accept the gift of his grace.

I also want her to know eternity waits for all of us. It simply

The Miracle of Kayla

comes down to choosing to live eternity in heaven by accepting the gift of God's love through Jesus Christ or to live eternity in hell by rejecting his gift. I pray every day she chooses correctly and that I did everything I could do to help her choose wisely. It has now become the burden I feel on my heart for every man, woman, and child. God placed that burden on my heart as I started to write this book. Another blessing I never saw coming.

He placed in my heart the desire to tell this story. It is not my story, Nancy's story, or even Kayla's story. It is God's story. I tell it to anyone who will listen. I will tell it until the day he takes me home. Only now do I understand how God took the threads of my life — my early childhood, my career, the trials and tribulations of our struggle with infertility, our life-shattering miscarriage, the devastating adoption fraud, and the day I held my daughter for the first time — and wove them into the tapestry of my life. Yet, I also know my life is entwined into the lives of others. He is weaving into one grand design the tapestry of all our lives until he reveals his final masterpiece in the fullness of his time.

And now I have told my small part in his masterpiece to you. Is there a story he is writing in your life? Perhaps he is writing it right now. If he is, trust me, it will be a great story. God is not limited by trying to "think outside the box." After all, he is the Author of creation, and we have the honor of being the characters in his book.

AFTERWORD

In the first sentence following the opening words of the "Lord's Prayer," Jesus taught his disciples to pray,

"your kingdom come, your will be done, on earth
as it is in heaven." (Matt 6:10)

In *The Miracle of Kayla*, our inclination is to think this story centers on Kayla, or her parents, Dan and Nancy, or their seven-year adoption journey filled with joy and heartache, triumph and despair. A deeper look, however, reveals that on every page, the hero of the story is a good and gracious God who desires for every individual to seek after, to know, and to follow his perfect will for his or her life.

Dan and Nancy had such a strong desire to have a child. The story pulsates with that yearning, but even stronger, is their commitment to trust God, come what may, knowing that his way and his will are always right … even when, unexpectedly, life seems to be going so horribly wrong. Indeed, this loving, ordinary couple found that the will of an extraordinary God is the knot you hang on to when you find yourself at the end of the rope.

"But, how do I know God's will for my life?" I've either asked that question or been asked that question hundreds of times over the past 40 years. In 35 years of ministry, suffice it to say that may very well be the number one issue people are grappling with when they come in for spiritual guidance.

From my own experiences of searching and through the study of God's Word, coupled with years of trying to help others, I have come to the place of understanding that discerning God's will is not meant to be complicated. In fact, I'm afraid that, at times, the simple phrase, "searching for God's will," implies he is hiding it from us. Quite the contrary — God wants us to know his will for our lives even more than we want to know it. He simply wants us to take the first step of desiring to know it, and follow it, with all our hearts.

Starting there, finding God's will has one more crucial step: make sure you're committed to obeying what you already know to be God's will. The Bible is filled with scriptures that instruct us to do something and then it says, "for this is the will of the Father." If we will follow those simple admonitions, we will quickly discover God revealing his will to us.

That is the DNA of Dan, Nancy and Kayla's truly amazing journey. As their pastor, I have had the joy, week in and week out, of worshipping and serving with this family. Their story challenges and inspires you, but, most of all, they desire for this story to point you to the love and grace of the one true God, through his Son, Jesus Christ, and his great plan for your life.

Dr. Doug Melton

Daniel J. Williams

ABOUT THE AUTHOR

After a long career serving his country, Daniel Williams retired from the FBI. He remains very active with the martial arts, working out and giving speeches on a variety of topics. He enjoys teaching Vacation Bible School to young children. Despite receiving numerous awards and holding many titles during his distinguished FBI career, the title he treasures the most is "Daddy."

CPSIA information can be obtained
at www.ICGtesting.com
Printed in the USA
BVHW03*1114080718
521068BV00007B/29/P